Maths

10 Minute Tests

9-10 years

Test 1: **Shape and Space**

Test time: 0 – 5 – 10 minutes

1

Which of these shapes is an octagon? Circle the answer.

A B C
D E

2

Jemma arrives at Gina's house at 1 pm.
She leaves $5\frac{1}{2}$ hours later.
What will the time be on a 24-hour clock?

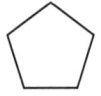

3

Using the grid, write down the coordinates of points A and B.

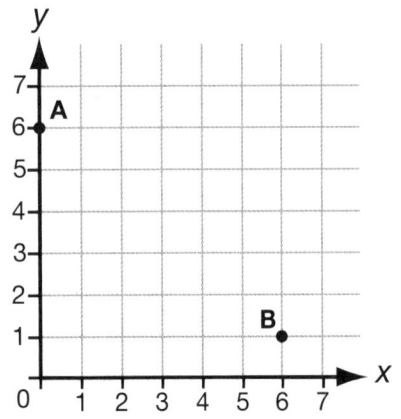

A _____
B _____

4

Draw the reflection of this shape in the line of symmetry.

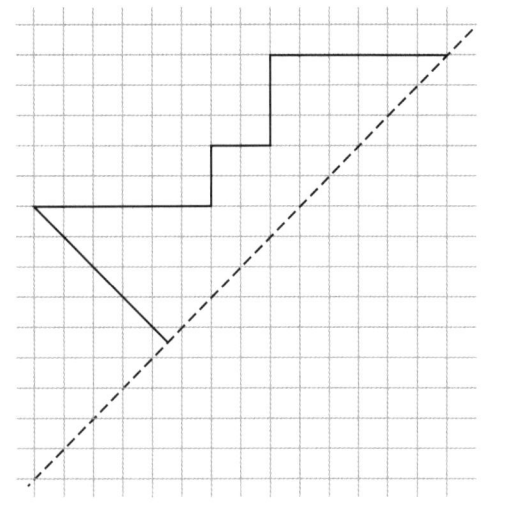

5

How many grams does the sugar weigh?

_____ g

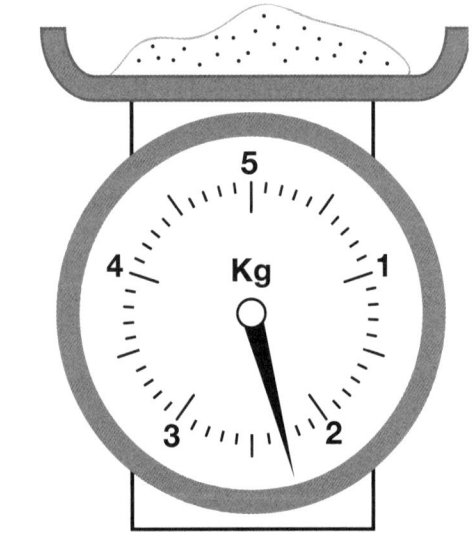

6
What is the perimeter of this shape?

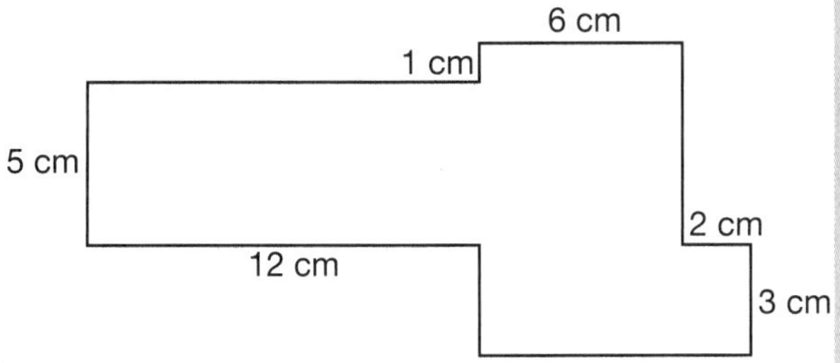

Perimeter = _____ cm

7
Look at the nets above. Which net makes a cube?
Circle the answer.

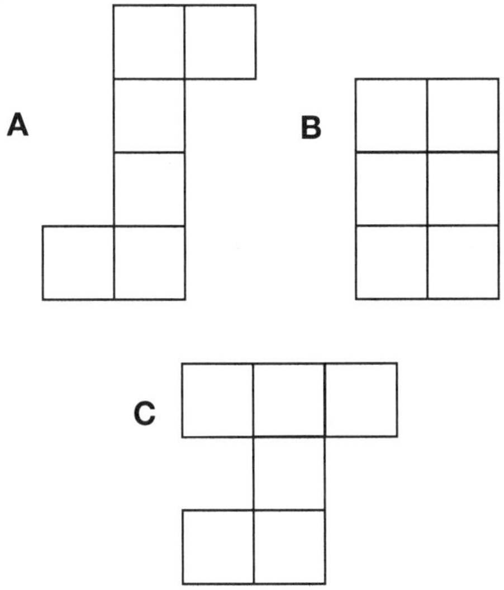

8
Which two angles would lie exactly along a straight line?
Circle the answer.

A 123° and 56°   B 125° and 56°
C 123° and 57°   D 121° and 57°
E 125° and 57°

9
How many millimetres lie between the arrows?
Circle the answer.

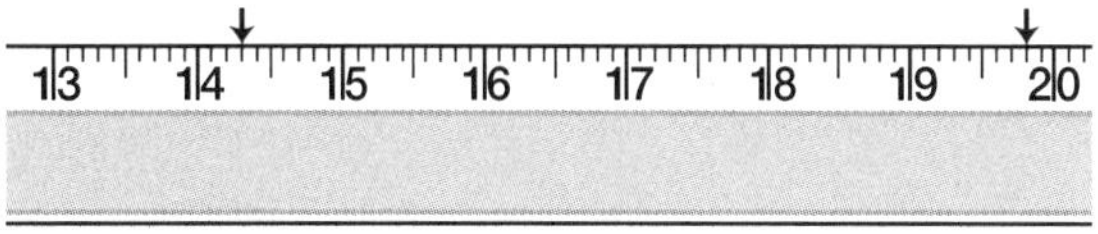

A 35 mm
B 40 mm
C 45 mm
D 50 mm
E 55 mm

10
Which two lines are perpendicular to each other?
Circle the answer.

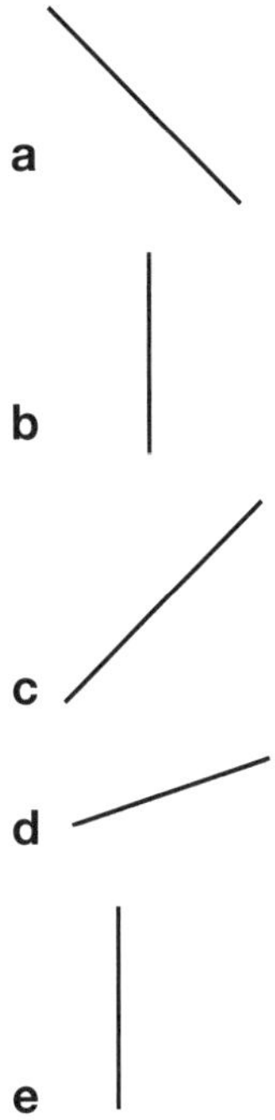

A a and b   B a and c   C b and e
D d and e   E b and d

TEST 2: Number

Test time: 0 — 5 — 10 minutes

1 Circle the equivalent fraction of $\frac{3}{7}$.

A $\frac{4}{5}$ B $\frac{7}{10}$ C $\frac{6}{14}$

D $\frac{5}{8}$ E $\frac{6}{9}$

2 Put these numbers in order, smallest first.

−2   1   −5   5   −1

____ ____ ____ ____ ____

3 What is one hundredth of 7000?
Circle the answer.

A 7
B 17
C 70
D 170
E 700

4 Write the answer.

15 × 23 = _____

5 Divide 67 000 by 1000. _____

6 454 783

What is the digit 5 worth in this number?
Circle the answer.

A Five units
B Five tens
C Five hundreds
D Five thousands
E Fifty thousands

7 An aeroplane has to fly 11 635 miles to Sydney, Australia.
It refuels after 6530 miles. How many more miles does it have to travel?

_____ miles

8 Underline the longer distance.

23 891 m   **23 981 m**

9 Write the missing number in this sequence.

32   25   18   11   ____   −3   −10

10 A number is multiplied by itself.
The answer is 64. What is the number?
Circle the answer.

A 1   B 8   C 16
D 32   E 46

TEST 3: **Shape and Space**

Test time: 0 — 5 — 10 minutes

1
Complete the following sentence.

This 3-D shape has _____ faces, _____ vertices and _____ edges.

2
How many days are there in a leap year? Circle the answer.

A 356 **B** 365
C 366 **D** 370
E 376

3
If a tennis ball lies midway between the basket ball and the football, what are its coordinates?

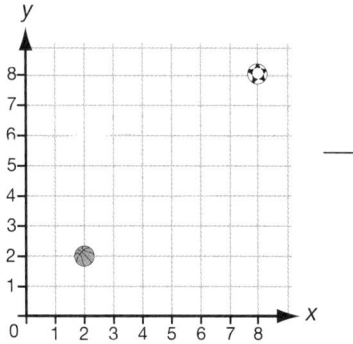

_____

4
How many lines of symmetry does this shape have?
Circle the answer.

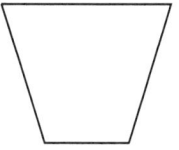

A 0   **B** 1
C 2   **D** 3
E 4

5
How many millilitres are there in 1.1 litres?
_____ mℓ

6
What is the approximate area of a rectangle 5.8 cm by 4.1 cm?
Circle the answer.

A 9cm²   **B** 10 cm²   **C** 20 cm²
D 24 cm²   **E** 99 cm²

7
Is this angle **acute** or **obtuse**?

_____

8
Which 3-D shape can you make from this net?

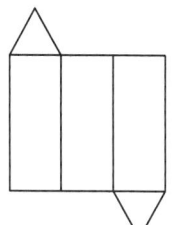

_____

9
Which unit of measure would you use to find the area of a stamp? _____

10
Draw a polygon with two sets of parallel lines.

Test 4: Data Handling

Test time: 0 — 5 — 10 minutes

1

The table below shows the goals scored by Haughton Wanderers over a seven week period.

Week 1	Week 2	Week 3	Week 4	Week 5	Week 6	Week 7
4	2	4	3	3	4	5

What is the mode? _____

2

Circle the word that most closely matches this statement.

'It will rain at some time in September in the UK'

IMPOSSIBLE
UNLIKELY
LIKELY
CERTAIN

3

Class 5's Favourite meal

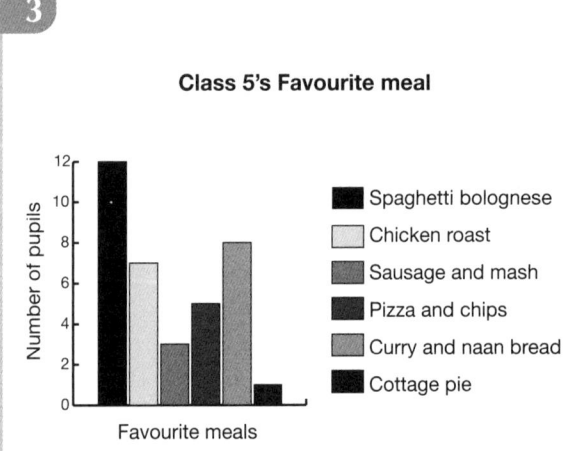

- Spaghetti bolognese
- Chicken roast
- Sausage and mash
- Pizza and chips
- Curry and naan bread
- Cottage pie

Which is Class 5's least favourite meal?

_____

4

In the vehicle survey, there were twice as many cars as lorries and a total of 27 vehicles.

Complete the frequency table to show this information.

Survey of vehicles passing the school between 10 am and 10.30 am		
Vehicles	Tally	Total
Bus	‖	2
Lorry		
Car	卌 卌 ‖	12
Bike		

5

One of these statements about England is UNLIKELY. Circle it.

A It will rain during May.

B The temperature will be hot during December.

C Leaves will be blown from the trees in October.

D It will be sunny in London in August.

E During every season it will rain.

6-7

The table below shows the weight gained by Oscar's puppy during the first six months of its life.

Draw a line graph to show this data.

Month	May	Jun	Jul	Aug	Sept	Oct
Weight gained (kg)	0.5	1.1	2.3	3.3	5	6.2

8-9

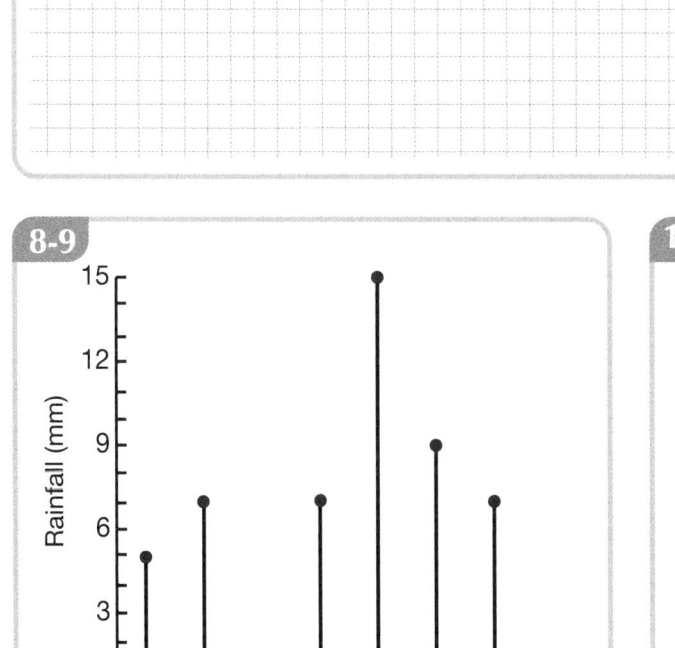

How much rain fell during this week?
_____ mm

What is the difference in mm between the days with the least and most rainfall?

_____

10

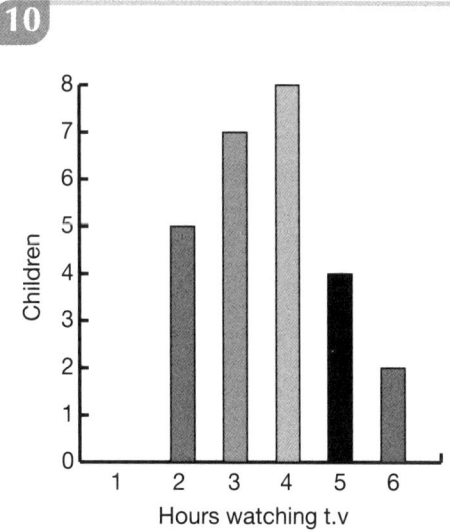

How many children watched three or more hours of television?

Circle the answer.

A 7   **D** 21

B 12   **E** 26

C 18

Test 5: Number

Test time: 0 – 10 minutes

1 Circle the number that equals 7 × 7
61   52   43   31   49   39

2 Subtract 56.4 from 81.23
_____

3 Daniel was given £5.60.
He spent half of the money.
How much did he have left?

£ _____

4 Circle a pair of factors for 24.
A 2 and 14   B 3 and 7   C 5 and 6
D 5 and 8   E 3 and 8

5 Hussain was on holiday for 4 days.
What fraction of a week is this?
Circle the answer.

A $\frac{1}{2}$ B $\frac{1}{3}$ C $\frac{3}{7}$ D $\frac{4}{5}$ E $\frac{4}{7}$

6 Mum made some cakes to sell at the school fete. Each cake needed 3 eggs. Mum used 36 eggs. How many cakes did she make?
Circle the answer.

A 3
B 6
C 12
D 33
E 108

7 Continue the pattern.
2.4   2.7   3.0   ___   ___

8 Jenny got 73 out of 100 for her spelling test.
What percentage did Jenny get?
Circle the answer.

A 7%   B 7.3%   C 70%   D 73%   E 100%

9 Which decimal is the same as $2\frac{6}{10}$?
Circle the answer.

A 2.66   B 2.06   C 2.16   D 2.6   E 2.1

10 Round 4555 to the nearest 100.
_____

Total

TEST 6: Data Handling

Test time: 0 — 5 — 10 minutes

1-2

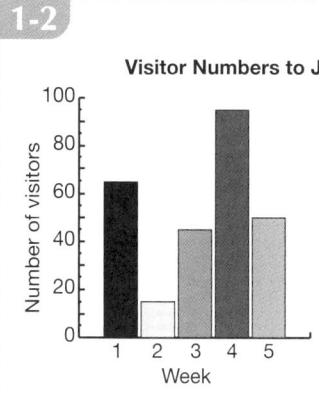

In which week might the weather have been poor? _____

During which week was it half-term holidays? _____

3-4

In this survey of pocket money, 27 children were asked how much they received each week.

Complete this frequency table.

Survey of pocket money given each week		
Amount of money	Tally	Total
£10.00	I	1
£5.00	III	3
£4.50	I	1
£4.00	IIII	5
£2.00		
£1.50	IIII	5

How many children received over £4.00 weekly? _____

5

Circle the word that most closely matches this statement.

'I can run faster than a train going at full speed.'

IMPOSSIBLE   **UNLIKELY**

LIKELY   **CERTAIN**

6-7

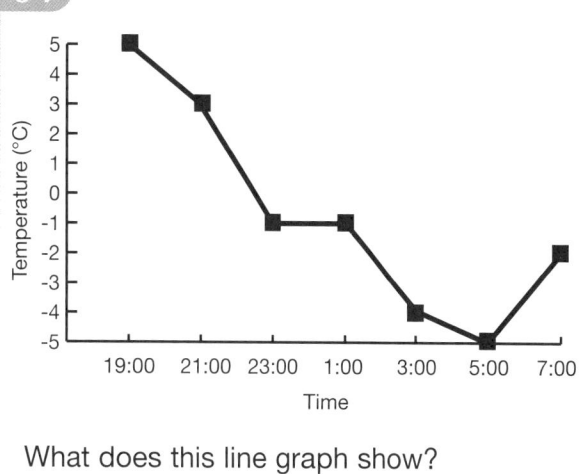

What does this line graph show?

_____

_____

_____

_____

Which interval has the biggest drop in temperature? _____

8-9

Ten friends compare their ages. Find the mode.

9   10   8   9   10   10   9   9   8   9

Mode = _____

Another ten children's ages are added to the survey. Does the mode change?

8   10   10   8   9   9   8   10   10   9

_____

10

Circle the word that most closely matches this statement.

'The sun will rise in the morning.'

IMPOSSIBLE   **UNLIKELY**

LIKELY   **CERTAIN**

Time for a break! Go to Puzzle Page 42

TEST 7: Shape and Space

Test time: 0 — 5 — 10 minutes

1
Name a 3-D shape with five faces, where four of the faces meet at one vertex.

_____

2
Draw the net of a cube.

3
Write 19 minutes to 5 in the afternoon on the 24-hour clock.

☐ : ☐

4-5
Plot and label the coordinates (2, 6), (7, 7), (3, 3), (4, 8) and (7, 3).

Then join the points.

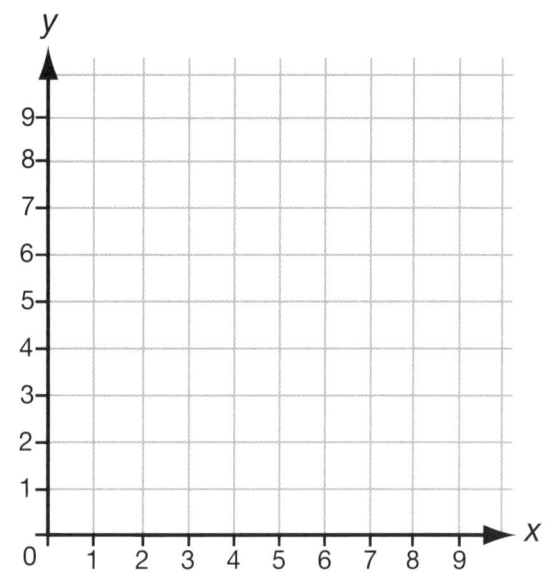

What shape have you drawn?

_____

6
Write two capital letters that have two lines of symmetry.

_____ _____

7

This jug contains 75 ml of juice. It needs one part juice to three parts water to make the drink.

Where will the liquid in the jug come to once the water is added?

Mark this on the jug.

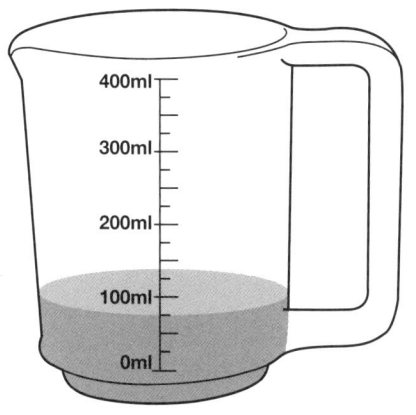

8

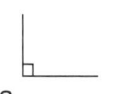 a   b   c

 d   e    f

 g   h

Which combination of angles are all obtuse?

Circle the answer.

A   a, c, d
B   c, d, h
C   b, e, g
D   a, f, g
E   d, f, h

9

9cm

15cm

What is the area of the rectangle?

_____ cm²

10

There are 1440 minutes in one day. How many minutes are there in a week?

Circle the answer.

A   10 080 minutes
B   14 400 minutes
C   100 100 minutes
D   10 800 minutes
E   10 400 minutes

Total

Test 8: Number

Test time: 0 – 5 – 10 minutes

1 How many more is 328 781 than 327 781?
_____

2 Fifty-six sweets were divided between 8 children. How many sweets did each child get?
Circle the answer.
A 3   B 4   C 7   D 8   E 9

3 Double 78. _____

4 75 out of 100 children at Towerwell Primary School walk to school.
What fraction of children walk to school?
Circle the answer.
A $\frac{1}{5}$ B $\frac{1}{3}$ C $\frac{1}{2}$ D $\frac{2}{3}$ E $\frac{3}{4}$

5 Complete the sequence correctly.
124   111   ____   85   ____   59

6 Which two numbers would complete this number sentence?
Circle the answer.
78 = ____ + ____
A 39, 41   B 29, 49   C 36, 41
D 27, 52   E 67, 15

7 Write a decimal fraction between 6.7 and 6.8
_____

8 Write the number seventy-eight thousand and seventy-eight.
_____

9 Tom's Dad drove 32 miles each day, travelling to and from work.
He worked Monday to Friday. How many miles did he drive in total?
Circle the answer.
A 150
B 160
C 170
D 180
E 190

10

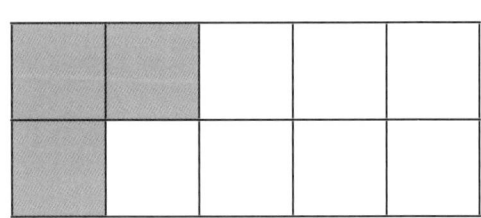

What percentage of the shape is shaded?
_____%

Total

TEST 9: Shape and Space

1

Three vertices of a square are plotted at (3, 2), (6, 2) and (6, 5). What are the coordinates of the fourth vertex?

_____

2-3

Use this bus timetable to answer the questions.

Reading Central	16:30	17:35	18:40
Caversham	16:42	17:47	18:52
Emmer Green	16:55	18:00	19:05
Reading Bridge	17:15	18:20	19:25

If you were picked up in Caversham at 17:47 how long would your journey to Reading Bridge take?

_____ minutes

What time will the next bus after 19:05 stop at Emmer Green? _____

4

Which shape has only one line of symmetry? Circle the answer.

A   B   C   D   E

5

A bag of potatoes weighs 400 g. If the bag could hold 1 kg of potatoes, what percentage of the bag is 400 g?
Circle the answer.

A 10%   B 20%   C 40%   D 60%   E 80%

6-7

If the perimeter of a square is 48 cm, what is the length of each of its sides?

_____ cm

What is the area of this square?
Circle the answer.

A 48 cm²   B 148 cm²   C 120 cm²

D 144 cm²   E 140 cm²

8

Calculate the missing angle on this straight line.

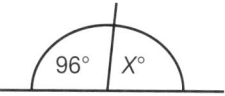

_____°

9

Which of these is an isosceles triangle?

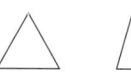   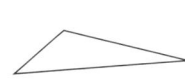

A   B   C   D

10

Approximately how many litres will a small fish tank for 3–5 goldfish hold?
Circle the answer.

A 1 litre

B 2 litres

C 25 litres

D 250 litres

E 2500 litres

Test 10: Number

Test time: 0 — 5 — 10 minutes

1-2

A local farmer bought 72 sheep. He split them equally between four fields.
How many sheep did he put in each field?
_____

A month later he bought some more sheep. He now owned 88 sheep.
How many more sheep were put into each of the four fields?
_____

3

Which is the smallest fraction?
Circle the answer.

$\frac{1}{2}$ $\frac{3}{5}$ $\frac{7}{10}$ $\frac{1}{4}$ $\frac{2}{5}$ $\frac{2}{10}$

4

Write a number above 10 and less than 20 that is a multiple of 2, 3 and 6.
_____

5

The temperature in a conservatory is 7°C. Overnight it falls by 12°C.
What does the temperature fall to?
Circle the answer.

A −5
B 0
C 5
D 7
E 19

6

Round 24.79 to the nearest whole number.
_____

7

Tessa runs 100 metres in 1 minute exactly. Jana runs the same distance 15 seconds quicker than Tessa. How many seconds does Jana run the distance in?
Circle the answer.

A 15   B 30   C 45   D 60   E 75

8

What sign is missing from this number sentence?
Circle the answer.

720 ? 16 = 45

A +   B −   C ×   D ÷

9

Write this number to two decimal places.
5.67219 _____

10

Work out 327 × 6 _____

14

Total

Test 11: **Problem Solving**

Test time: 0 — 5 — 10 minutes

1
Find a number for each shape.

□ + ◯ + ⬡ = 2

□ = _____

◯ = _____

⬡ = _____

2
How much change would you be given from £1.00 if you bought nine sweets at 9p each?

_____ p

3
Mrs Golding's class are going on a theatre trip. Parents are providing the transport. There are 33 children going and each parent can take 4 children in a car. How many parents are needed to help?

Circle the answer.

A 4
B 6
C 8
D 9
E 12

4-5
At a firework display, 212 litres of soup are sold in aid of the local school. Each cup of soup holds 250 ml and costs £1.25

How many cups of soup are sold?

_____

How much money is raised?

£ _____

6
Aimee lets her guinea pigs out in their grass run at 07:50 each day and puts them away at 17:25. How long do the guinea pigs spend outside?

_____

7
The Lee family are on a touring holiday. So far they have travelled 1156 miles and have filled the petrol tank four times. How many miles are they travelling on each tank of fuel?

Circle the answer.

A 260   B 289   C 310   D 362   E 400

8
What is the number I am thinking of?
When I add 14 to the number then divide by 9, the answer is 9. What is the number?

Circle the answer.

A 18   B 23   C 67   D 81   E 126

9
Geraint collects 185 conkers. He divides the conkers equally between himself and four of his friends. How many conkers do they each get?

Circle the answer.

A 35   B 36   C 37   D 38   E 39

10
What is the missing sign? Write it in the star.

315 ☆ 63 = 5

Test 12: Data Handling

1

What is the likelihood that the following statement will come true?

Circle the answer.

'There will be a traffic jam somewhere in the country today.'

IMPOSSIBLE **UNLIKELY**
LIKELY **CERTAIN**

2

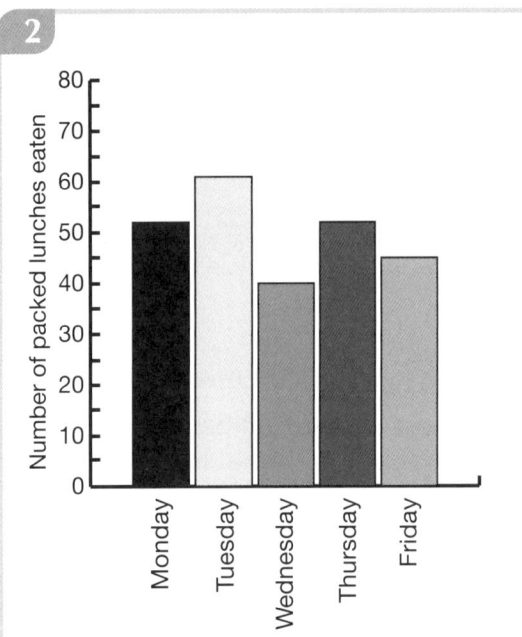

On which days did the same number of children eat packed lunches?

_____ _____

3

What is the chance the following statement will happen? Circle the answer.

'Someone in my class will win an Olympic gold medal.'

A GOOD CHANCE

B POOR CHANCE

C NO CHANCE

4

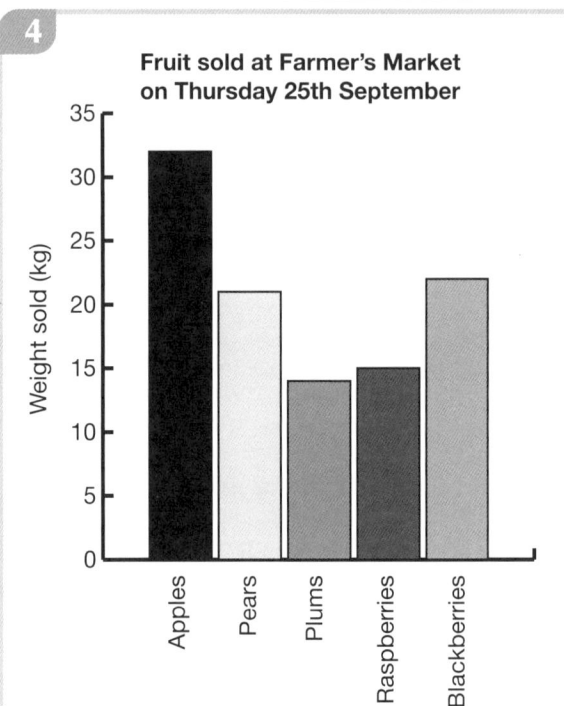

Which fruit was the farmer's poorest seller? Circle the answer.

A apples

B pears

C plums

D raspberries

E blackberries

5

Look at this frequency table.

Survey of favourite television programmes		
Programme	Tally	Total
Dr Who	|||| |||| |||| |||| |||	23
Tracey Beaker	|||| |||| ||||	15
Blue Peter	|||| |||| |||| ||	17
Newsround	||||	5

How many children were surveyed? Circle the answer.

A 40 **B** 45 **C** 50 **D** 55 **E** 60

6-7

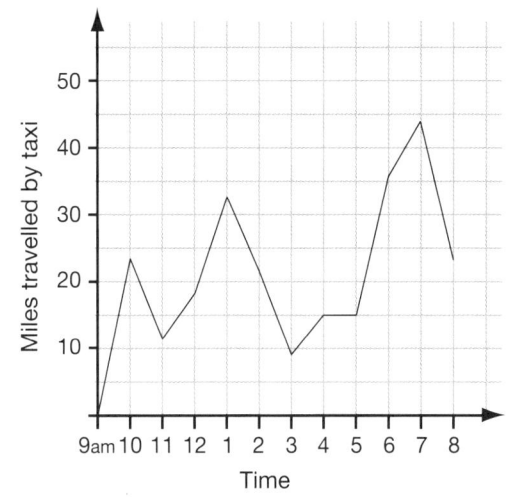

Describe what this line graph is showing.
_____
_____

Why do you think the taxi was busier between 6 pm and 8 pm than between 9 am and 11 am?
_____
_____

8

The following are the results of a spelling test. It was out of 10.

7 8 7 6 9 9 8
7 9 7 9 2 9 8

What is the mode? _____

9-10

Every morning break at Moreton Primary School, children are offered an apple as a snack. This table shows how many apples were eaten in the first week of term.

Monday	43
Tuesday	32
Wednesday	36
Thursday	20
Friday	29

How many apples were eaten during the week? _____

The following week only 119 apples were eaten.

How many more apples were eaten in the first week compared to the second?

_____

Time for a break! Go to Puzzle Page 43 ▶

Total

Test 13: **Number**

Test time: 0 — 5 — 10 minutes

1 An egg box holds 6 eggs. How many egg boxes are needed for 90 eggs?

_____

2 What is 15% of £60? Circle the answer.

A £5
B £9
C £15
D £30
E £45

3 Which of the following is 3479 rounded to the nearest 10, 100 and 1000?
Circle the answer.

A 3480, 3500, 4000
B 3470, 3400, 3000
C 3480, 3500, 3000
D 3480, 3400, 3000
E 3470, 3500, 4000

4 Write these numbers in descending order.

67 893   45 231   67 992
45 321   67 450

_____ _____ _____
_____ _____

5 Write in words the number 79 830.

_____
_____

6 How many quarters are there in $12\frac{3}{4}$? Circle the answer.

A 25   B 51   C 50   D 49   E 27

7 Fill in the space in this number sentence.

6700 ÷ _____ = 67

8 What temperature is shown on this thermometer?

_____ °C

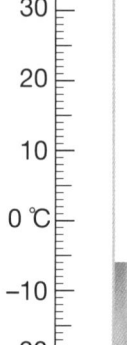

9 Jess reads 17 pages of her reading book each night. How many pages does she read in 26 nights?
Circle the answer.

A 107   B 249   C 378   D 442   E 450

10 56   39   22   5   −12

What is the rule for this sequence?

_____
_____

Total

Test 14: Problem Solving

Test time: 0 — 5 — 10 minutes

1

In this calculation the same digit is missing from three places. Circle the value for the missing digit.

● ● 8 − 3 ● 2 = 106

A 9   B 7   C 6   D 5   E 4

2

If all the ages of the Rowland family are added together the total is 108 years. Dad is 43. He is two years older than Mum. Finn is a third of Alice's age. She is 12. Tom's age lies exactly between Alice and Finn's ages. Find the missing ages.

Mum = _____   Tom = _____

Finn = _____

3

Raj thinks of a number. He multiplies it by 8 and the answer is 208.

What was his number? Circle the answer.

A 20   B 26   C 28   D 128   E 200

4

Hannah was sending her Christmas cards. She needed twelve 25p stamps, three 45p stamps and five 63p stamps. How much did the stamps cost her in total?

£ _____

5

Write a number story for:

110 × 29 = 3190

_____

_____

_____

6

Jake bought a 4 kg bag of carrots to feed to his ponies. He gave them 800 g a day. How many days did the bag of carrots last? Circle the answer.

A 1   B 3   C 5   D 7   E 9

7

Which three consecutive numbers total 666?

_____   _____   _____

8

George has collected 134 stickers out of the 520 needed to complete the book. How many more stickers does George need to collect to have half the stickers? Circle the answer.

A 90

B 116

C 126

D 130

E 260

9-10

On Monday a florist buys 42 bunches of flowers to sell in her shop. She sells 35 of these bunches for £3.99 each.

How much money does she take?

£ _____

The next day the florist puts in a second order. This brings the total number of bunches she has to sell on Tuesday to 50. How many more bunches did she have to order?

_____

Total

Test 15: Shape and Space

1
Daniel spent three weeks preparing and writing a presentation on whales.

He began work on the project on the 15th May. What date did he finish the project?

_____

2
Complete this table with equivalent measures.

500 ml	0.5 l
25 cm	m
200 g	kg
100 m	km

3
Draw the time found on the 24-hour clock on the clock face.

21:41

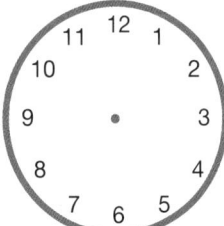

4
Which item will weigh approximately 35 kg? Circle the correct answer.

A an acorn

B a medium-sized dog

C a car

D a chicken

E a house brick

5
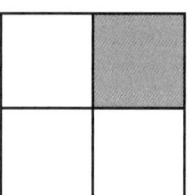

The perimeter of the whole square is 32 cm.

What is the perimeter of the shaded square? _____ cm

6
Translate this shape 4 units to the right.

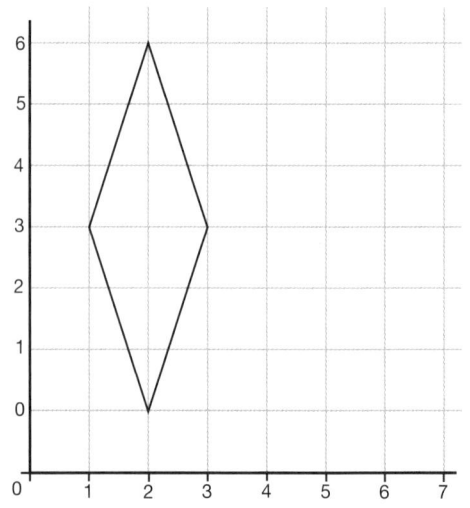

7

Draw two lines of symmetry on this shape.

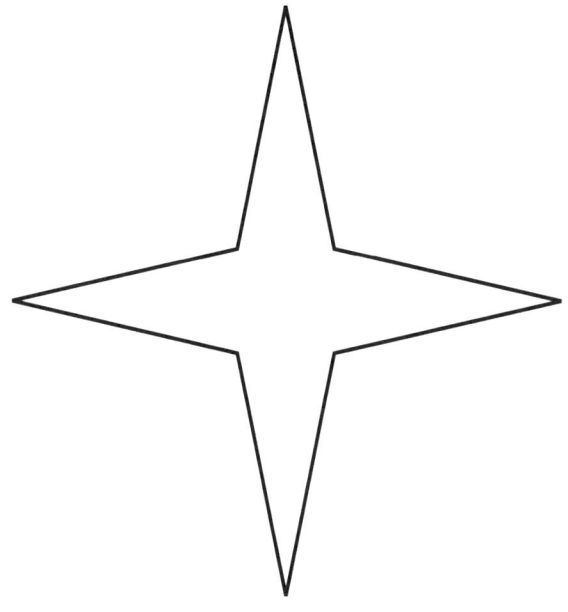

Are there more than two lines of symmetry?

Circle the answer.

Yes / No

8

Which two angles add together to make a right angle?
Circle the answer.

A 56° and 23°
B 90° and 90°
C 102° and 78°
D 95° and 85°
E 48° and 42°

9

Which of the following options correctly lists the coordinates of all four points?

Circle the answer.

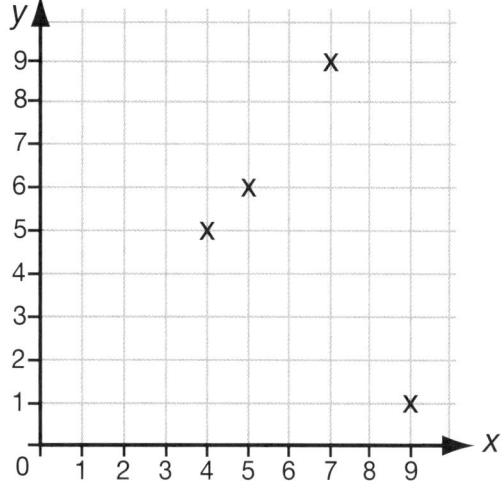

A (4, 5) (6, 5) (7, 9) and (9, 1)

B (4, 5) (5, 6) (7, 9) and (1, 9)

C (4, 5) (5, 6) (7, 9) and (9, 1)

D (5, 4) (5, 6) (7, 9) and (9, 1)

E (4, 5) (5, 6) (9, 7) and (9, 1)

10

Name a 3-D shape with only three faces.

_____

Test 16: Mixed

Test time:

1

What is 5663 to the nearest 100?
Circle the answer.

A 5600
B 5700
C 6600
D 6700
E 5650

2

Using the grid, write down the coordinates of Q.

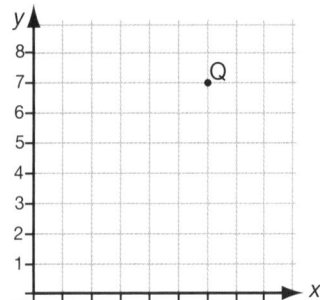

Q _____

3

Complete the calculation correctly.

553 − _____ = 427

4

The Balfour family were leaving early to catch the plane to Trinidad.

They went to bed at 8.30 pm. Their alarm woke them 5 hours 16 minutes later.

Write the time they were woken on the 24-hour clock.

5

Look at this line of beads. What colour will the 19th bead be? _____

6

How many thirds are there in $7\frac{2}{3}$? _____

7

Calculate the missing angle on this straight line.

_____ °

8

The perimeter of this square is 56 cm. What is the length of one side?

_____ cm

9

$9^3 =$ _____

10

Is the number 53 a prime number or a composite number?

_____

Test 17: Mixed

1 Write the pairs of factors of 24.

___ and ___   ___ and ___
___ and ___   ___ and ___

2 How many lines of symmetry does this shape have? ___

3 Rewrite these numbers in ascending order.

56 233   123 783   56 232   123 793

___   ___   ___   ___

4 Write this number as a decimal.

$12\frac{3}{4}$ = ___

5 Look at this line graph.

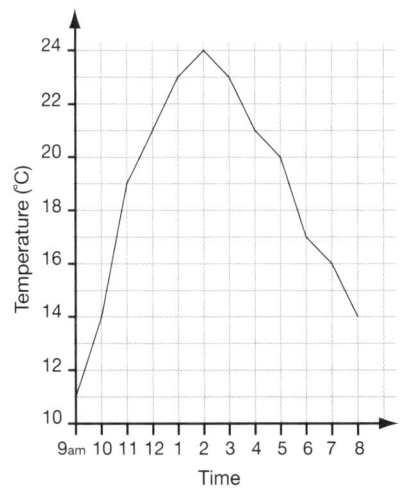

Between which times did the temperature fall at its quickest rate? ___ and ___

6 Two numbers have the sum of 57. One number is 19. What is the other number? Circle the answer.

A 7   B 18   C 24   D 38   E 76

7 Write the rule explaining this sequence.

133   122   111   100   89   78   67

___
___
___

8 Tom is going to France for a day trip. He has been given £25 to spend. How many euros will he get for £25?

£1 = 1.4 euros

£25 = ___ euros

9 Approximately how much does an apple weigh?
Circle the answer.

A 1 kg   B $\frac{1}{2}$ kg
C 25 g   D 100 g
E 500 g

10 What kind of triangle is this?

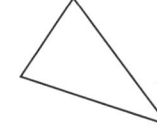

___

TEST 18: **Mixed**

Test time: 0 – 10 minutes

1

Class 1	☆	☆	☆	☆		
Class 2	☆	☆	☆			
Class 3	☆	☆				
Class 4	☆	☆	☆	☆	☆	
Class 5	☆	☆	☆			

Key: ☆ stands for 4 children having school dinners

Look carefully at the pictogram. Describe in a sentence or two what it is showing.

_____
_____
_____
_____
_____

2

9 3 6 1 8 4 7

Rearrange these digits to make the smallest whole number you can.

_____

3

Find the total area of Laura's stable block.

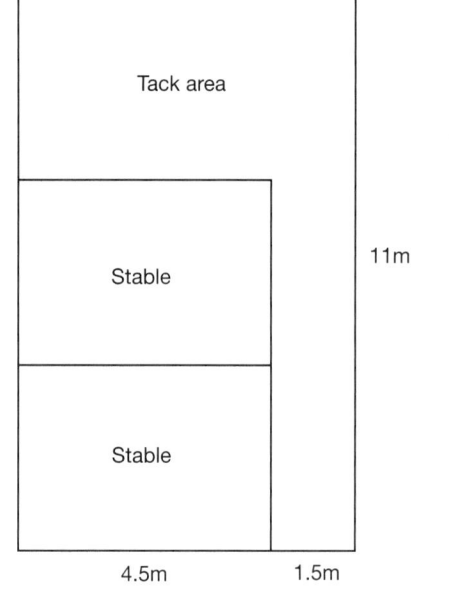

Area = _____ m^2

4

Class 3, made up of 17 boys and 19 girls, were visiting a Roman villa on a school trip. Their class teacher decided she wanted to buy each of her pupils a memento of the trip. She bought each child a pencil costing 25p. How much did it cost her?

Circle the answer.

A £3   **B** £6   **C** £9   **D** £12   **E** £15

5

Write the number 93 618 in words.

_____
_____
_____

Test 1: Shape and Space (pp 2–3)

1 **A** An octagon is a 2D shape with 8 faces.
2 **18:30** Add 5 hours to 1 pm (= 6 pm). ½ hour is 30 minutes, so add this on (= 6.30 pm). To change analogue time into the 24-hour clock, add 12 to the hours from 1 pm to 11pm: 6 + 12 = 18.
3 **A(0, 6), B(6, 1)** To make sure the coordinates are written in the correct order, use the phrase 'Along the corridor and up the stairs'. 'Along the corridor' refers to the numbers along the *x* axis, so this number is first. 'Up the stairs' refers to the numbers going up the *y* axis, so this number is second.
4
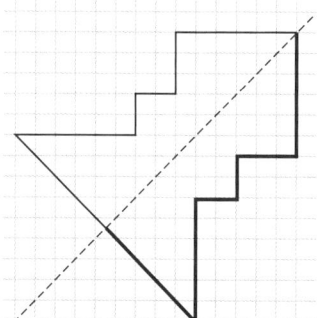

The dotted line shows the line of symmetry and a mirror image (reflection) of the shape is needed on the other side of this line.
5 **2300** 1 kg = 1000 g so change the kilograms into grams by multiplying by 1000. The weight on the scales is just over 2 kg = 2000 g. Each kilogram on the scales is separated into 10 equal parts: 1000 g ÷ 10 = 100 g. The weight shown on the scales is at the third mark after 2 kg: 3 × 100 g = 300 g. 2000 g + 300 g = 2300 g.
6 **58** The perimeter of a shape is the total length around the outside. To find the missing lengths, separate the shape into 3 rectangles.

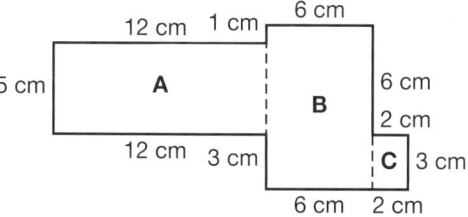

Use the measurements given on the opposite sides to calculate the missing measurements. The missing measurement at the bottom left of rectangle B will be 3 cm, the same as that shown opposite on rectangle C. The missing length on the right side of rectangle B will be the same as the sum of 5 cm and 1 cm on the opposite sides: 5 cm + 1 cm = 6 cm. The bottom of rectangle B will be 6 cm and the bottom of rectangle C will be 2 cm. Choose a starting point and add all the measurements together:
12 + 1 + 6 + 6 + 2 + 3 + 2 + 6 + 3 + 5 + 12 = 58 cm.
7 **A** Copy and cut out the nets shown, then assemble each to find which one can create a cube.
8 **C** Angles along a straight line always add up to 180°: only the angles given in option C add up to 180°.
9 **E** The numbers on the ruler represent centimetres and the small lines between each centimetre represent millimetres. 1 cm = 10 mm so convert the centimetres into millimetres by multiplying by 10: 14 cm × 10 = 140 mm. The first arrow is pointing to the third increment after 14: 140 mm + 3 mm = 143 mm. The second arrow is pointing to the eighth increment after 19: 19 cm × 10 = 190 mm; 190 + 8 = 198 mm. Subtract to find the difference: 198 − 143 = 55 mm.
10 **B** Perpendicular lines are at right angles (90°) to one another. Only options A and C would be perpendicular if joined together.

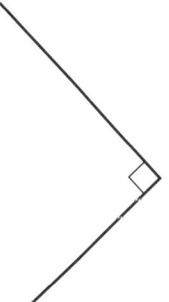

Test 2: Number (p 4)

1 **C** To find an equivalent fraction, both numbers in the fraction must be multiplied or divided by the same number. When a number is divided, it is also called 'simplifying'. No number can divide into both 3 and 7 to create a new fraction, so multiply each number by 2, then 3 and so on. The only equivalent fraction shown is $\frac{6}{14}$.
$\frac{3 \times 2}{7 \times 2} = \frac{6}{14}$
2 **−5, −2, −1, 1, 5** Negative numbers 'mirror' whole numbers, as shown below. Write the numbers on a number line to help put them in order.

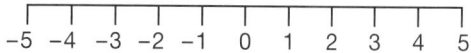

3 **C** To find one hundredth of a number, divide by 100. To divide by a power of 10, place the numbers in a decimal grid with hundreds, tens, units, tenths, hundredths, etc. Divide a number by moving it to the right of the decimal point: count the zeros in the number you are dividing by to find how many places to move it. There is one zero in 10, so move the number one place to the right; there are two zeros in 100, so move it 2 places; three zeros in 1000, so move it 3 places and so on. Here, there are 2 zeros in 100, so the number needs to be moved 2 places to the right: 70.00 is the same as 70.

1000s	100	10s	Units	Decimal Point	1/10ths	1/100ths
7	0	0	0	•		
		7	0	•	0	0

4 **345** Use long multiplication to complete the calculation: first, multiply 23 by the 5 in the units column; then, in the row below, place a zero in the units column and multiply 23 by the 1 in the tens column; finally, add the two answers together (115 + 230 = 345).

```
      2 3
  ×   1 5
  1 1 1
  1 1
+ 2 3 0
  3 4 5
```

5 **67** Refer to Q3 on dividing by powers of ten.

6 **E** Write the numbers in a place value grid, as shown. The 5 is in the 'ten thousands' column: 50 000 = fifty thousands.

10,0000s	10,000s	1000s	100	10s	Units
4	5	4	7	8	3
	5	0	0	0	0

7 **5105** Use column subtraction to find the answer. Work from right to left and make sure the number in the next column is borrowed from if the number above it is smaller.

```
   0⁺ ¹1 6 3 5
  −   6 5 3 0
      5 1 0 5
```

8 **23 981 m** Place both numbers in a place value grid and compare each digit in turn starting from the left. If the two digits are the same, go on to the next column.

10,000s	1000s		100	10s	Units
2	3		8	9	1
2	3		9	8	1

9 **4** Find the difference between two adjacent numbers to find how to continue the sequence. The numbers decrease by 7 each time, so subtract 7 to find the missing number: 11 − 7 = 4 and check with 4 − 7 = −3. Refer to the number line shown in Q2 with negative numbers and use this to count back on.

10 **B** Use knowledge of times tables to multiply each of the numbers by itself to find the answer: 8 × 8 = 64.

Test 3: Shape and Space (p5)

1 **6 faces, 8 vertices and 12 edges** A face is a flat surface on one side of a 3D shape; an edge is where two faces meet; a vertex is the point where three or more edges (or faces) meet. The plural of vertex is vertices.

2 **C** There are 365 days in a normal year: a leap day has one extra day (29th February), so the answer is 366.

3 **(5, 5)** Refer to Test 1 Q3 on coordinates. Count the number of squares on the *x* axis from the basket ball (2, 2) to the football (8, 8). There are 6 squares between them, so half of 6 (3) is the midway point: count on 3 squares along the *x* axis from the basket ball to find the first number = 5. Repeat by counting up the *y* axis to find the midway point going upwards: the number along the y axis is also 5.

4 **B** For a shape to have a line of symmetry, both sides either side of the dotted line need to be a mirror image of one another.

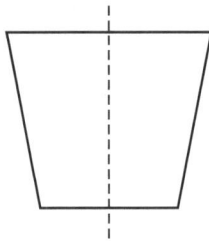

5 **1100** 1 litre = 1000 ml so change the litres into millilitres by multiplying by 1000. To multiply by a power of 10, place the numbers in a place value grid with hundreds, tens, units, tenths, etc. Multiply a number by moving it to the left of the decimal point: count the zeros in the number to find how many places to move it. To multiply by 10 move it one place to the left; by 100, move it two places; by 1000, move it three places; and so on. Add a zero in the units, tens, hundreds, etc, if they are left empty.

1000s	100	10s	Units	Decimal Point	1/10ths
			1	•	1
1	1	0	0	•	

6 **D** To find the area of a rectangle, multiply the length by the width. Round each decimal number to the nearest whole number to find the approximate answer: if the digit after the decimal point is between 0 and 4, then the number to the left of the decimal remains the same; if the digit after the decimal is between 5 and 9, then the digit to the left of the decimal increases by 1. 5.8 cm is rounded to 6 cm and 4.1 cm is rounded to 4 cm: 6 × 4 = 24 cm.

7 **acute** An acute angle is less than 90° and an obtuse angle is greater than 90°, but less than 180°.

8 **triangular prism** Copy and cut out the net shown, then assemble to find the 3D shape. A prism has two ends that are the same shape; the name of this shape tells you the type of prism it is. Each end is a triangle so this is a triangular prism.

9 **mm** Millimetres are smaller than centimetres, so will give a more accurate measurement.

10 A polygon is a shape with at least 3 sides and angles. Parallel lines are lines which are always the same distance apart; they never meet or cross.

Test 4: Data Handling (pp 6–7)

1 **4** The mode is the number that occurs the most often.

2 **LIKELY** In probability, if the statement refers to something that can happen, without any doubt, the answer is CERTAIN. If it cannot ever happen, the answer is IMPOSSIBLE. If it has a small chance of happening, then it is UNLIKELY; if it has a strong chance of happening, the answer is LIKELY. LIKELY is the best option here as it is a definite possibility, but not certain.

3 **Cottage Pie** Each bar is shown in a different colour: use the key on the right to find out which bar represents which meal. The numbers 0–12 going up the side of the graph show the number of pupils; the least favourite meal is shown by the shortest bar. The bar for cottage pie is the shortest, showing only 1 pupil.

4 First, find the number of lorries. 'There were twice as many cars as lorries' and the table shows there were 12 cars: 12 ÷ 2 = 6 lorries. The total number of vehicles is 27, so add the number of buses, lorries and cars (2 + 6 + 12 = 20) and subtract the answer from 27 to find the number of bikes (27 − 20 = 7 bikes). To complete the tally column, vertical lines are used to keep count; 4 vertical lines are crossed with one diagonal line every time 5 is reached.

Survey of vehicles passing the school between 10 am and 10.30 am		
Vehicles	**Tally**	**Total**
Bus	||	2
Lorry	ⅢⅠ |	6
Car	ⅢⅠ ⅢⅠ ||	12
Bike	ⅢⅠ ||	7

5 **B** Refer to Q2 on probability.

6–7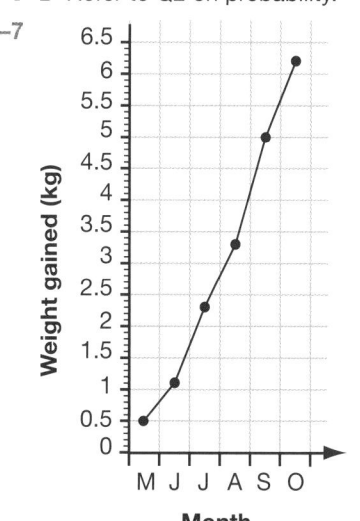

Begin by writing the months along the bottom at regular intervals (these can be abbreviated to show the first letter only). Then add the numbers to show the weight going up the side of the graph: the weight ranges from 0.5 to 6.2, therefore it would be best to show the weight in intervals of 0.5 (from 0 to 6.5 or 7 kg) using the boxes on the grid. Each of these boxes can then be divided by 5 to show increments of 0.1. Mark each of the measurements on the graph and then join them together to create the line graph.

8–9 **50, 15** To find how much rain fell on each day, follow the line up from the day on the x axis and make a note of the number the dot at the end of the line is level with (the lines go up by 1 each time, with every third number shown). The rainfall was: Tuesday 5 mm, Wednesday 7 mm, Thursday 0 mm, Friday 7 mm, Saturday 15 mm, Sunday 9 mm and Monday 7 mm. Add them together to find the total: 5 + 7 + 0 + 7 + 15 + 9 + 7 = 50 mm. The day with the least rainfall was Thursday (0 mm) and the day with the most rainfall was Saturday (15 mm): 15 − 0 = 15.

10 **D** Look at the bars for 3, 4, 5 and 6 hours and check the numbers they are level with: 3 hours = 7 children, 4 hours = 8 children, 5 hours = 4 children and 6 hours = 2 children. Add the number of children together: 7 + 8 + 4 + 2 = 21 children.

Test 5: Number (p 8)

1 **49**

2 **24.83** Use column subtraction to find the answer. Line the decimals up so that they are in the same column and make sure the larger number is at the top. Place a decimal in the answer space, aligned with the others, to make sure it is in the correct place in the answer. There will be an empty space after the number 56.4, so add a zero to make sure both numbers have the same amount of digits (56.40 is the same as 56.4). Work from right to left and borrow from the top number in the next column if the number above it is smaller.

```
  ⁷8  ¹⁰4  •  ¹2  3
-  5   6  •   4  0
   2   4  •   8  3
```

3 **2.80** Use short division to complete the calculation. To halve the number, divide by 2: 2 into 5 goes 2 times with a remainder of 1, so write 2 above the 5 and carry the 1 over to the next column to create the number 16; 2 goes into 16 eight times, so write 8 above the 6; 2 goes into 0 zero times, so write 0 above the zero in 5.60.

```
    2  •  8   0
2 | 5  •  ¹6  0
```

4 **E** A factor is a number that can be divided into another number exactly. For example, 1, 2, 3 and 6 are factors of 6. Only 3 and 8 divide into 24 without leaving a remainder.

5 **E** There are 7 days in a week and Hussain was on holiday for 4 out of 7 days, which can be written as $\frac{4}{7}$.

6 **C** Divide 36 by 3 to find the answer. Refer to Test 5 Q3 on short division or use knowledge of times tables to invert the calculation; 3 × 12 = 36, so 36 ÷ 3 = 12.

7 **3.3, 3.6** Refer to Test 2 Q9 on sequences and Test 5 Q2 on column subtraction. Or write the decimal numbers on a number line and count the decimal points between the numbers shown.

2.4 2.5 2.6 2.7 2.8 2.9 3.0 3.1 3.2 3.3 3.4 3.5 3.6

8 **D** Percent means per 100 so a percentage is a number out of 100: 73 out of 100 is 73%.

9 **D** Refer to Test 2 Q1 on equivalent fractions. Convert $\frac{6}{10}$ to a fraction with a denominator of 100 by multiplying both numbers by 10 to give $\frac{60}{100}$; the top number will then be the first two digits after the decimal point (0.60 is the same as 0.6). Or, convert the fraction into a decimal by dividing the top number by the bottom number. Use short division to do this (refer to Test 5 Q3). Add a decimal point after the numerator (top number) in the calculation and keep adding zeros if any numbers need to be carried over: 6 ÷ 10 = 0.6. The whole number (2) remains the same and 2 + 0.6 = 2.6.

```
      0  •  6
10 | 6  •  ⁶0
```

10 **4600** To round numbers to the nearest 10, 100, 1000, etc., look at the digit in the following place value column (use the place value grid shown in Test 2 Q3): round down if it is 4 or less and round up if it is 5 or greater. When rounding to the nearest hundred, look at the digit in the tens column: 4555 is rounded up to 4600 because 5 in the hundreds column is rounded up to 6 and the tens and units both become 0.

Test 6: Data Handling (p 9)

1–2 **Week 2, Week 4** To find the amount of visitors for each week, follow each bar upwards to see which number on the y axis it is level with. Week 2 shows the fewest visitors (15) and fewer people are likely to visit a garden when the weather is poor. More people would be able to visit during a school holiday and Week 4 shows the most visitors (95).

3–4

Survey of pocket money given each week		
Amount of money	Tally	Total
£10.00	|	1
£5.00	|||	3
£4.50	|	1
£4.00	||||	5
£2.00	|||| |||| ||	12
£1.50	||||	5

5 To complete the table, add all the numbers in the column showing the total number of children (1 + 3 + 1 + 5 + 5 = 15) and subtract this from 27 to find how many children were given £2.00 per week (27 − 15 = 12 children). To find how many children received <u>over</u> £4.00, add the total number of children who received £4.50, £5.00 and £10.00: 1 + 3 + 1 = 5 children. To complete the tally column, vertical lines are used to keep count; 4 vertical lines are crossed with one diagonal line every time 5 is reached.

5 **IMPOSSIBLE** Refer to Test 4 Q2 on probability.

6–7 ***The line graph shows the change in temperature through one night and the early hours of the next morning.*** **21:00 to 23:00** To find the biggest drop in temperature, use the numbers showing the temperature to count on and find the difference between each of the temperatures that decrease. The temperature decreases the most between 21:00 and 23:00, where it drops by 4° (from 3° to −1°).

8–9 **9, No** The mode is the number that occurs the most often.

10 **CERTAIN** Refer to Test 4 Q2 on probability.

Test 7: Shape and Space (pp 10–11)

1 **Square-based pyramid** A 3D shape which has more than one face meeting at a vertex will be a pyramid. Four faces meet at the vertex, which means the shape at the bottom of the pyramid will have four faces – a square; therefore a square-based pyramid is being described. Refer to Test 3 Q1 on faces.

2 The following are examples. When the net is assembled, the cube must have 6 faces.

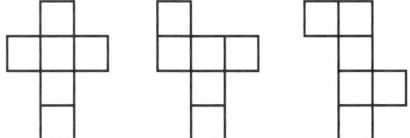

3 **16:41** There are 60 minutes in an hour, so subtract 19 from 60 to find the minutes: 60 − 19 = 41. The time is 'minutes to' 5, so the hour has not yet reached 5 and is still 4. Refer to Test 1 Q2 on changing analogue time to the 24-hour clock: 4 + 12 = 16, so the hour is 16. Write the hours followed by the minutes: 16:41.

4–5 Refer to Test 1 Q3 on coordinates.

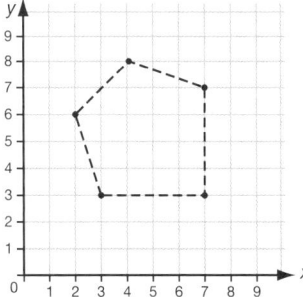

Pentagon A five sided shape is called a pentagon.

6 **H, I, O or X** Refer to Test 3 Q4 on symmetry.

7 ***300 ml marked on jug*** The drink needs to be calculated in a ratio of one part juice to three parts water, a ratio of 1 : 3. Add the numbers in the ratio to find the total number of parts (1 + 3 = 4) and multiply the answer by 75 ml: 4 × 75 = 300.

8 **B** Refer to Test 3 Q7 on acute and obtuse angles. Angle f is greater than 180° so it is a reflex angle.

9 **135** To find the area of a rectangle, multiply the length by the width. Use column multiplication, carrying over to the next column when needed.

$$\begin{array}{r} 1\ 5 \\ \times\ \ \ \ 9 \\ \hline 1\ 3\ 5 \\ {\scriptstyle 4} \end{array}$$

10 **A** There are 7 days in one week so multiply 1440 by 7. Refer to Q9 on column multiplication.

Test 8: Number (p 12)

1 **1000** Refer to Test 2 Q7 on column subtraction: 328 781 − 327 781 = 1000.

2 **C** Use knowledge of times tables and invert the calculation; 8 × 7 = 56, so 56 ÷ 8 = 7.

3 **156** Partition the number into 70 and 8. Double 70, then double 8 and add the answers together: 70 × 2 = 140; 8 × 2 = 16; 140 + 16 = 156.

4 **E** Refer to Test 2 Q1 on equivalent fractions. 75 out of 100 is the same as $\frac{75}{100}$ and both numbers can be divided by 25 to simplify the fraction to $\frac{3}{4}$.

5 **98, 72** Refer to Test 2 Q9 on sequences. 13 has been subtracted each time.

6 **B** Add the numbers in each of the options to find the correct answer. A quick way to do this is to look at the units: only option B has units which will give 8 units in the answer.

7 ***One of the following: 6.71, 6.72, 6.73, 6.74, 6.75, 6.76, 6.77, 6.78 or 6.79*** A decimal fraction is a fraction that has a denominator of 10, 100, 1000, etc. so can be written as a decimal number. For example, $\frac{15}{100}$ can be written as the decimal fraction 0.15. Decimal numbers increase in the same way as whole numbers. For example, 0.1 is followed by 0.2, 0.3, 0.4 and so on and 0.01 is followed by 0.02, 0.03, 0.04 and so on.

8 **78 078** Write the numbers in the place value grid shown on Test 2 Q8 to help write the number in words.

9 **B** Monday to Friday is 5 days, so multiply 32 by 5. Refer to Test 7 Q9 on column multiplication.

10 **30** 3 out of 10 squares have been shaded, the fraction $\frac{3}{10}$. To change a fraction into a percentage, the denominator (bottom number) needs to be 100. Multiply both the numerator and the denominator by 10 to change them to 30 and 100, respectively. The new fraction is $\frac{30}{100}$ which = 30%.

Test 9: Shape and Space (p13)

1. **(3, 5)** A square has sides of equal length so two of the first digits in the coordinates will be the same and two of the second digits in the coordinates will be the same. (6, 2) and (6, 5) both have 6 as the first number and the other one, (3, 2), has 3, so the first digit in the answer must be 3. (3, 2) and (6, 2) both have 2 as the second digit and the remaining one, (6, 5), has 5, so the second digit in the missing coordinate must be 5.

2–3. **33, 20:10** Calculate the number of minutes from 17:47 to the next hour: there are 60 minutes in an hour so subtract 47 from 60: 60 – 47 = 13 minutes. There are 20 minutes between the next hour 18:00 and 18:20. 13 + 20 = 33 minutes. To find the time of the next bus, find the difference between times of the buses shown for Emmer Green. Count up to the next hour from 16:55 to 17:00 to find a difference of 5 minutes, then count up from 17:00 to 18:00 to find a difference of 1 hour. Count on this amount from 19:05: 19:05 + 1 hour = 20:05; 20:05 + 5 minutes = 20:10.

4. **D** Refer to Test 3 Q4 on symmetry.

5. **C** Convert 1 kg into grams by multiplying by 1000. 400 out of 1000 is the same as the fraction $\frac{400}{1000}$. Refer to Test 8 Q10 on changing a fraction into a percentage: $\frac{400}{1000} = \frac{40}{100}$, which is 40%.

6–7. **12, D** A square has 4 equal sides: 48 cm ÷ 4 = 12 cm. Refer to Test 3 Q6 on finding the area of a rectangle (a square is a regular rectangle): 12 cm × 12 cm = 144 cm².

8. **84** Angles along a straight line always add up to 180°: 180° – 96° = 84°.

9. **B** An isosceles triangle has 2 angles the same size and 2 sides the same length.

10. **C** Think about measurements of items such as a large bottle of water (1.5 or 2 litres) to help decide on the most appropriate answer. 1 litre and 2 litres will not be enough and 250 litres and 2500 litres will be too much, so the most appropriate answer is 25 litres.

Test 10: Number (p14)

1–2. **18, 4** Refer to Test 5 Q3 on short division. 72 ÷ 4 = 18. Then subtract 72 from 88 to find out how many more sheep he bought: 88 – 72 = 16; 16 ÷ 4 = 4, so 4 more were put in each field.

3. $\frac{2}{10}$ To compare fractions, find a number that all the denominators will divide into, without leaving a remainder: 2, 5, 10 and 4 can all divide into 20. Find the equivalent of each fraction by multiplying the numerators (top number) by the same number the denominator has been multiplied by. For example, $\frac{1}{2}$ becomes $\frac{10}{20}$, $\frac{3}{5} = \frac{12}{20}$, $\frac{7}{10} = \frac{14}{20}$, $\frac{1}{4} = \frac{5}{20}$, $\frac{2}{5} = \frac{8}{20}$ and $\frac{2}{10} = \frac{4}{20}$. $\frac{4}{20}$ is the smallest fraction, the equivalent of $\frac{2}{10}$.

4. **12 or 18** A multiple is a number that can be divided by another number without leaving a remainder. Use knowledge of the times tables to find the answer. Find the multiples of the largest number first: multiples of 6 between 10 and 20 are 12 and 18. 12 and 18 are also multiples of 2 and 3, so either of these are an acceptable answer.

5. **A** Use a number line (see Test 2 Q2) to count back from 7 and find the answer –5.

6. **25** Refer to Test 3 Q6 on rounding decimals to the nearest whole number.

7. **C** 1 minute is 60 seconds and 60 – 15 = 45.

8. **D** One of the four operations (+, –, × and ÷) needs to replace the mark. If the answer is greater than the numbers in the calculation; it will be an addition or multiplication. If the answer is less than the numbers in the calculation, then it will be a subtraction or division. 720 – 16 = 704, so it cannot be subtraction, therefore 720 ÷ 16 = 45.

9. **5.67** A number with 2 decimal places has two digits after the decimal point. Refer to Test 3 Q6 on rounding.

10. **1962** Refer to Test 7 Q9 on column multiplication.

Test 11: Problem Solving (p15)

1. Knowledge of decimals adding up to 1 whole is needed. For example, just as 8 + 2 = 10, then 0.8 + 0.2 = 1. Possible answers could be 1 + 0.8 + 0.2 = 2 or 1 + 0.4 + 0.6 and so on. Each shape is different so each number needs to be different as well.

2. **19** Use knowledge of times tables to find 9 × 9 = 81p. £1.00 is the same as 100p, so subtract 81 from 100 using column subtraction. Work from right to left and use borrowing if needed. When borrowing from zero, always change it into a 9 and borrow from the next column instead.

$$\begin{array}{r} ^{0}\!\!\not{1}\ ^{9}\!\!\not{0}\ ^{1}0 \\ -\ \ \ 8\ \ 1 \\ \hline 1\ \ 9 \end{array}$$

3. **D** Use knowledge of times tables to find how many times 4 can go into 33: 4 × 8 = 32. This means 8 cars will be completely full with 4 children each, but another car will be needed for the remaining child, so 9 cars are needed.

4–5. **848, 1060.00** There are 1000 ml in 1 litre. 1000 ml ÷ 250 ml = 4 cups of soup so 212 litres × 4 cups = 848 (see Test 7 Q9 on column multiplication). Multiply 848 cups of soup by £1.25 (using column multiplication again) to find how much money is raised = £1060.00.

6 **9 hours 35 minutes** This is quite a long length of time so it would be best to count on from 07:50 to 17:25 using a number line, remembering there are 60 minutes in 1 hour. 07:50 to 08:00 is 10 minutes; 08:00 to 17:00 is 9 hours; 17:00 to 17:25 is 25 minutes. Add all the times calculated together: 10 minutes + 9 hours + 25 minutes = 9 hours 35 minutes.

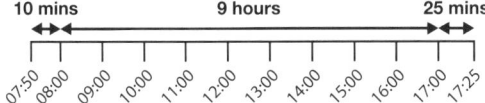

7 **B** See Test 5 Q3 on short division. 1156 ÷ 4 = 289.
8 **C** Write out the calculation as a missing number sentence: □ + 14 ÷ 9 = 9. Work backwards through the equation completing the inverse (multiply instead of dividing, subtract instead of adding, etc): 9 × 9 = 81 and 81 – 14 = 67.
9 **C** Refer to Test 5 Q3 on short division. 185 ÷ 5 = 37
10 **÷** Refer to Test 10 Q8 on completing calculations with missing operations. 315 ÷ 63 = 5

Test 12: Data Handling (pp 16–17)

1 **LIKELY** See Test 4 Q2 on probability.
2 **Monday and Thursday** Look for two bars of the same height: only Monday and Thursday show the same number (50).
3 **B** Refer to Test 4 Q2 on probability. GOOD CHANCE is the same as LIKELY; POOR CHANCE is the same as UNLIKELY; and NO CHANCE is the same as IMPOSSIBLE.
4 **C** Look for the shortest bar on the chart: plums sold the least amount.
5 **E** Add the numbers in the column showing the total: 23 + 15 + 17 + 5 = 60.
6–7 *The line graph shows the number of miles travelled by a taxi throughout a day.*
For example, the taxis could have been busier in the evening compared to the morning because a number of people called on taxis in the evening, rather than drive their own cars.
8 **9** The mode is the number that occurs the most often.
9–10 **160, 41** Add the number for each day: 43 + 32 + 36 + 20 + 29 = 160.
160 – 119 = 41 (See Test 2 Q7 on column subtraction).

Test 13: Number (p 18)

1 **15** Refer to Test 5 Q3 on short division. 90 ÷ 6 = 15
2 **B** Find 10% by dividing £60 by 10 = £6. Half of 10% is 5%, so halve £6 to find 5% = £3. Add £6 + £3 to find 15%: £6 + £3 = £9.
3 **C** Refer to Test 5 Q10 on rounding.
4 **67 992, 67 893, 67 450, 45 321, 45 231** Refer to Test 2 Q8 on comparing numbers. The numbers need to be written in descending order, so the largest one is first, the smallest one is last.
5 *Seventy-nine thousand, eight hundred and thirty* Write the numbers in a place value grid like in Test 2 Q6 to help write the number in words.
6 **B** There are 4 quarters in 1 whole, so there are 48 quarters in 12 (4 × 12 = 48). Add the 3 quarters shown in the fraction to 48 to get the answer: 48 + 3 = 51.
7 **100** Invert the calculation to help find the answer: 6700 ÷ ____ = 67 is the same as 6700 ÷ 67 which gives 100. See Test 5 Q3 on short division.
8 **–6** Refer to Test 2 Q2 on negative numbers.
9 **D** Refer to Test 2 Q4 on long multiplication. 17 × 26 = 442
10 **Number decreases by 17 each time.** Refer to Test 2 Q9 on sequences.

Test 14: Problem Solving (p 19)

1 **E** Use logic and estimation to select the most appropriate number: for example, the first digit in the second number is 3 (3•2) and only 4 can have 3 subtracted from it to get the answer of 1. Check with column subtraction (refer to Test 2 Q7): 448 – 342 = 106.
2 **Mum = 41, Tom = 8, Finn = 4** Mum is 2 years younger than dad who is 43 and 43 – 2 = 41. For Finn, divide Alice's age by 3: 12 ÷ 3 = 4, so Finn is 4. Tom's age is halfway between Finn's age (4) and Alice's (12), therefore 8. Add all the ages together to check they add up to 108: 43 + 41 + 4 + 12 + 8 = 108.
3 **B** The calculation is □ × 8 = 208, which can be inverted to 208 ÷ 8 to find the answer. See Test 5 Q3 on short division. 208 ÷ 8 = 26
4 **7.50** Use long multiplication (see Test 2 Q4) and column multiplication (see Test 7 Q9) to complete the calculations 25p × 12 = 300p; 45p × 3 = 135p; and 63p × 5 = 315p. Add the totals together using column addition. Work from right to left and make sure any numbers that are carried over are added on in the next column.

```
    3  0  0
    1  3  5
 +  3  1  5
 ─────────
    7  5  0
          1
```

100p = £1.00 so divide 750p by 100 to find the answer of £7.50. Refer to Test 2 Q3 on dividing by powers of ten.
5 *Child's own number story for 110 × 29 = 3190, e.g. Liz collected 110 stamps for 29 weeks so*

at the end of the time she had 3190 stamps.
6 **C** 1 kg = 1000 g, so 4 kg = 4000 g. To divide 4000 g by 800 g, remove the same amount of zeros from each number to get the calculation 40 ÷ 8 (= 5). Or use repeated addition to keep adding lots of 800, until the number 4000 is reached: 800 + 800 + 800 + 800 + 800 = 4000; 5 lots of 800 have been added together.
7 **221, 222 and 223** Three consecutive numbers are needed so divide 666 by 3: 666 ÷ 3 = 222. Subtract 1 from 222 to get 221 and add 1 to get 223. Check by adding the numbers together: 221 + 222 + 223 = 666.
8 **C** Halve 520 to find how many stickers he needs to have half: 520 ÷ 2 = 260 (see Test 5 Q3 on short division). Then subtract the 134 stickers he already has: 260 − 134 = 126 (refer to Test 2 Q7 on column subtraction).
9–10 **139.65, 43** Round £3.99 to £4.00 to make the calculation easier. 35 × £4 = £140 (see Test 7 Q9 on column multiplication). 35 lots of 1p were added when rounding, so subtract 35p (£0.35) from £140 to find the answer of £139.65 (refer to Test 2 Q7 on subtracting decimal numbers). Subtract the 35 bunches she sold from the 42 bunches she originally had: 42 − 35 = 7 left. Then subtract 7 from 50 to find how many she would have had to order: 50 − 7 = 43.

Test 15: Shape and Space (pp 20–21)

1 **4th June** There are 7 days in a week and 3 × 7 = 21, so 21 days need to be counted on. He began on 15th May, so this day needs to be included as well: there are 31 days in May and from 15th May to 31st May is 17 days. Subtract 17 from 21 to find how many days to count on in June: 21 − 17 = 4, so the answer is 4th June.
2 There are 100 cm in 1 m, so divide 25 cm by 100; there are 1000 g in 1 kg, so divide 200 g by 1000; there are 1000 m in 1 km, so divide 100 m by 1000. Refer to Test 2 Q3 on dividing by powers of ten.

500 mℓ	0.5 ℓ
25 cm	0.25 m
200 g	0.2 kg
100 m	0.1 km

3 To change 24-hour clock into analogue time, subtract 12 from hours between 13:00 and 23:00: 21 − 12 = 9, so the hour hand is on, or moving on from, the number 9 on the clock. For the minute hand, each number represents 5 minutes: 8 on the clock face represents 40 minutes past. The minute hand needs to be shown just after the 8 to show 41 minutes.

4 **B** Use knowledge of the weight of things you are familiar with to help choose the correct answer. For example, a bag of sugar weighs 1 kg, a car weighs around 1000 kg, etc.
5 **16** A square has 4 equal sides, so the length of each side is 32 ÷ 4 = 8 cm. The grey square is half the length of one side of the larger square, so each side of the grey square is 4cm. The perimeter of a shape is the total length around the outside: 4 + 4 + 4 + 4 = 16.
6 To translate a shape, move it without rotating or resizing it. Mark each vertex (corner) of the shape 4 squares to the right, then join them together using a ruler.

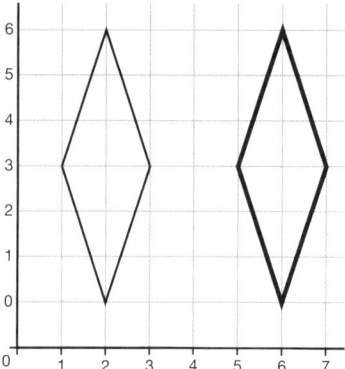

7 ***Two of the marked lines of symmetry.*** Refer to Test 3 Q4 on symmetry.

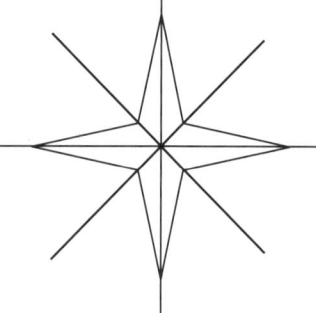

8 **E** A right angle is 90°. B, C and D already have angles greater than 90° so they are ruled out. Look at the units to see 56 and 23 can't add up to 90. The only two angles that have a total of 90° is 48° and 42°.
9 **C** Refer to Test 1 Q3 on coordinates.
10 ***cylinder*** A cylinder has 2 circular faces and a side between them which connects them together.

Test 16: Mixed (p 22)

1. **B** Refer to Test 5 Q10 on rounding.
2. **(6, 7)** Refer to Test 1 Q3 on coordinates.
3. **126** Invert the calculation to find the answer: 553 − ___ = 427 is the same as 553 − 427 = ___.
4. **01:46** Refer to Test 11 Q6 on calculating lengths of time. Begin by changing 8.30 pm into 24-hour clock by adding 12 to the hours: 8 + 12 = 20, so 8.30 pm is 20:30. Remember that the 24-hour clock finishes the day at 23:59, then begins the next day at 00:00. Use a number line to count on 5 hours and 16 minutes.

20:30 21:30 22:30 23:30 00:30 01:30 01:46

5. **white** The beads are in a sequence of 1 white, 2 black, 2 white, 1 black, then the sequence begins again. The sequence has a total of 6 beads, so use the six times table to count up in 6s, without going past 19: 3 × 6 = 18. Therefore the sequence will begin again on the 19th bead, so it will be white, the same as the first counter in the sequence.
6. **23** There are three thirds in 1 whole, so there are 21 thirds in 7 (3 × 7 = 21). Add the 2 thirds shown in the fraction to 21 to get the answer: 23.
7. **132** Angles on a straight line always add up to 180°, so subtract 48 from 180 to find the answer: X = 132°.
8. **14** The perimeter of a shape is the total length around the outside and a square has 4 sides of equal length, so divide 56 cm by 4. Refer to Test 5 Q3 on short division. 56 ÷ 4 = 14.
9. **729** 9^3 is 9 × 9 × 9. Work from left to right in the calculation 9 × 9 = 81 and 81 × 9 = 729. See Test 7 Q9 on column multiplication.
10. **prime number** A prime number is a number that can only be divided by the number 1 and itself. For example, 7 is a prime number as it can only be divided by 1 and 7 and 19 is a prime number as it can only be divided by 1 and 19. A composite number is a number that can be produced by multiplying other whole numbers together. For example, 6 is a composite number as it can be produced by multiplying 3 and 2 as well as 1 and 6.

Test 17: Mixed (p 23)

1. **1 and 24, 2 and 12, 3 and 8, 4 and 6** Refer to Test 5 Q4 on factors.
2. **2** See Test 3 Q4 on symmetry.
3. **56 232, 56 233, 123 783, 123 793** Refer to Test 2 Q8 on comparing numbers. The numbers need to be written in ascending order, which means the smallest one is first and the largest one is last.
4. **12.75** Refer to Test 5 Q9 on converting fractions into decimals. $\frac{3}{4}$ = 3 ÷ 4, which is 0.75. 12 is a whole number, so this remains unchanged to the left of the decimal point: 12 + 0.75 = 12.75.
5. **5 pm and 6 pm** Look for the steepest drop in temperature between each hour, shown by the line. The temperature dropped by 3° from 20° to 17° between 5 pm and 6 pm; it fell by 1° or 2° in the other hours.
6. **D** Write the calculation as a missing number sentence, then invert it: ☐ + 19 = 57, which is the same as 57 − 19 = ☐; 57 − 19 = 38.
7. **Number decreases by 11 each time.** Refer to Test 2 Q9 on sequences.
8. **35** When multiplying with decimal numbers, remove the decimal and complete the calculation as normal (refer to Test 2 Q4 on long multiplication). The number of decimal places in the answer will be the same as the number of decimal places in the original 25 × 1.4 has one digit after the decimal, so the answer will have one digit after the decimal as well. 350 becomes 35.0 (= 35.00) and therefore €35.00.

```
          2   5
    ×     1   4
    ─────────────
    1     0   0
          2
    + 2   5   0
    ─────────────
      3   5   0
```

9. **D** Use knowledge of the weight of things you are familiar with to help choose the correct answer. For example, a bag of sugar weighs 1 kg, the equivalent of 1000 g.
10. **isosceles** An isosceles triangle has 2 angles the same size and 2 sides the same length. Turn the page around to see this more clearly.

Test 18: Mixed (pp 24–25)

1. *The pictogram shows how many children in each class have school dinners. Each star represents 4 children and Class 4 has the most children (6 × 4 = 24) taking school dinners with Class 3 having the least children (2 × 4 = 8).*
2. **1 346 789** The smallest number will have the digits with the least value at the beginning, so write the digits in order, from smallest to largest.
3. **66** Use column addition to find the total width: 4.5 + 1.5 = 6. Align the decimals and work from right to left, making sure that any numbers that are carried over are added on in the next column. Multiply the length by the width to find the area of a rectangle: 11 × 6 = 66 m².

```
    4 . 5
+   1 . 5
    6 . 0
    1
```

4 **C** First, find the total number of pupils: 17 + 19 = 36. Then multiply 36 by 25p (refer to Test 2 Q4 on long multiplication). 36 × 25p = 900p. 900p = £9.00

5 **Ninety-three thousand, six hundred and eighteen.** To help write the number in words, use a place value grid as shown in Test 2 Q6.

6 Refer to Test 1 Q4 on drawing reflections.

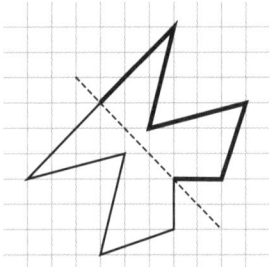

7 **D** Refer to Test 3 Q5 on multiplying by powers of 10. 3.6 kg × 1000 = 3600 kg

8 **B** A polyhedron is a 3D shape with flat faces. Each flat face is a polygon (a 2D shape with at least three sides or angles). A regular shape has all edges the same length.

9 **Approximately 300** To help estimate, either identify the halfway point on the line, which will be 250, or separate the line into five equal parts, labelling the first increment 100, then 200 and so on.

10 **88** Refer to Test 8 Q10 on changing a fraction into a percentage. Multiply both numbers by 2 to find the fraction $\frac{88}{100}$ and therefore 88%.

Test 19: Mixed (p 26)

1 **4.7** Make sure the number of millimetres are carefully counted after the number of centimetres shown: this gives the number after the decimal point.

2 **0.4** There are 1000 m in 1 km, so divide 400 by 1000. Refer to Test 2 Q3 on dividing by powers of ten.

3 **C** Divide 1260 by 9 to find how many lots of 9 are in 1260: 1260 ÷ 9 = 140. Refer to Test 5 Q3 on short division.

4 **E** Count on 7 days from 24th October makes Wednesday 31st October. Count on 2 more days to find 2nd November is a Friday.

5 $\frac{1}{3}$ There are 24 hours in a day and she spent 8 out of 24 hours at school, which can be written as $\frac{8}{24}$. This can be simplified to $\frac{1}{3}$ (see Test 2 Q1 on equivalent fractions).

6 **26°** Draw a number line, as shown on Test 2 Q2 and count from −8 to 18 to find the difference. Or, complete as a calculation 18 − −8. There are two minus signs next to one another; when two of the same signs are adjacent, they change to positive (+). Therefore the sum becomes 18 + 8 = 26.

7 **D** Use knowledge of the 8 times table. Refer to Test 10 Q4 on multiples.

8 *Child's own number story*, e.g., *When 237 sheep were split into 3 fields the farmer had 79 sheep in each field.*

9 **07:48 or 19:48** The hour hand has gone past the 7, but not yet reached the 8, so the hour is still 7. See Test 15 Q3 on counting minutes on a clock face: the minute hand has just passed the 9 = 45 minutes. The minute hand is pointing to the third interval after 45, so there are 48 minutes shown. This makes the time 07:48. See Test 1 Q2 on changing analogue time to the 24-hour clock. 19:48 is also an acceptable answer.

10 **D** A regular polygon is a shape that has 3 or more sides (or angles), all of which are the same. Only option D shows a shape with all sides and angles the same.

Test 20: Mixed (p 27)

1 **2, 47** Refer to Test 2 Q9 on sequences. The difference between 5 and 11 is 6 and the difference between 11 and 23 is 12, therefore the number added is doubled each time to form the sequence +3, +6, +12, +24 and +48.

2 $\frac{13}{5}$ To convert a mixed number into an improper fraction, convert the whole number into a fraction first: 2 wholes is $\frac{10}{5}$. Then add the fraction in the number: $\frac{10}{5} + \frac{3}{5} = \frac{13}{5}$ (when adding fractions, only the numerators (top numbers) are added, the denominator remains the same).

3–5 To keep count (tally), vertical lines have been used to keep count; 4 vertical lines are crossed with one diagonal line every time 5 is reached. To complete the total for Week 1 and 3, count the lines in the Tally column. For Week 2 and 4, convert the total shown into a tally, using vertical and diagonal lines as described.

Spelling test survey showing children in Class 5D with 90% or over		
Week	Tally	Total
1	✝✝ ❙❙	7
2	✝✝ ❙❙❙❙	9
3	✝✝ ✝✝	10
4	❙❙❙❙	4

Represent the number of children along the y axis: the highest total is 10 and 5 increments are shown, so the chart will go up in 2s. Label the axis to show it is representing the number of children. Draw bars extending upwards from the x axis and label each one to show the week number it represents. Week 1 will be level with 7 children (half-way between 6 and 8 on the chart), Week 2 will be level with 9 and so on. Finally, give the bar chart a title to explain what it is showing.

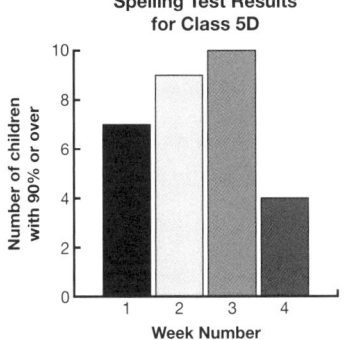

6 **6** Refer to Test 3 Q6 on finding the area of a rectangle. Original area: 7 × 3 = 21 m² and larger area: 9 × 3 = 27 cm². The difference is how much it was increased by: 27 − 21 = 6 m².

7 **(9 × 4) + 8 = 44** Two of the four operations (+, −, × and ÷) are missing from the calculation, If the answer is greater than the numbers in the calculation. it is more likely to be an addition or multiplication. If the answer is less than the numbers it, then it is more likely to be a subtraction or division. However, as the it involves brackets, this rule does not always apply so try different combinations. 44 is larger than 9, 4 and 8 so it would be best to begin by trying combinations of + and × to see if they work first. Remember to complete the calculation in the brackets separately: (9 × 4) + 8 is the same as (36) + 8.

8 **0.36** Use the place value column used in Test 2 Q3. Thirty-six hundredths can be written as $\frac{36}{100}$ and, as the denominator (bottom number) is 100, this can be transferred into the grid by writing the numerator (top number) after the decimal point. The number, when written in words, ends with 'six-hundredths' so write 6 in the hundredths place on the grid first, then work backwards, adding any numbers shown before it. Make sure a 0 is placed before the decimal point.

1000s	100	10s	Units	Decimal Point	1/10ths	1/100ths
			0	•	3	6

9–10 **acute, 29** An acute angle is less than 90°. Angles along a straight line always add up to 180°: 180° − 151° = 29°.

Test 21: Mixed (pp 28–29)

1 **B** Refer to Test 1 Q10 on perpendicular lines.
2 Refer to Test 15 Q6 on how to translate a shape.

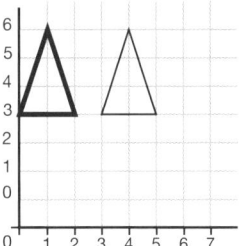

3 Refer to Test 1 Q3 on coordinates.

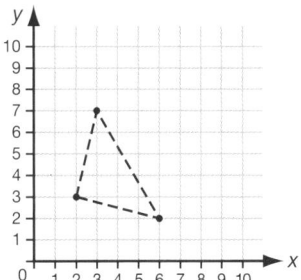

4 **right-angled triangle** The angle of the triangle shown at (2, 3) is a right angle, therefore it is a right-angled triangle.
5 **40** Refer to Test 11 Q8 on completing maths problems like this. ☐ ÷ 8 + 17 = 22; 22 − 17 = 5 and 5 × 8 = 40.
6 **e.g.**

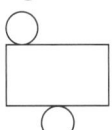

The net needs to show a rectangular shape, i.e., the middle of the cylinder, with two circles attached to it, the end faces of the cylinder.
7 **B** Refer to Test 3 Q4 on symmetry.
8 **April–May, 1.3** Each of the months is represented with its first letter along the x axis and the weight is shown on the y axis. Look for the steepest line between two months: April and May show the most amount lost between two months. There are 5 increments between each number on the y axis and the numbers shown increase by 0.5 each time. This means each increment between the numbers increases by 0.1 each time. The first weight shown is 99.9 and the last is 98.6. The difference is the total weight lost: 99.9 − 98.6 = 1.3 kg. Refer to Test 5 Q2 on subtracting decimal numbers.
9 **47.761** Refer to Test 7 Q9 on column multiplication. Align the decimal in the space for

the answer before completing the calculation, to make sure it is in the correct place, then complete it as normal.

```
     6 . 8 2 3
  ×          7
  4 7 . 7 6 1
      5 1 2
```

10 **Seven hundred and sixty-five thousand, five hundred and fifty-three.** The largest number will have the digits with the greatest value at the beginning, so write the digits in order from largest to smallest: 765553. Use the place value grid shown in Test 2 Q6 to help write the number in words.

Test 22: Mixed (p30)

1 **B** Refer to Test 2 Q2 on negative numbers. Count back 15 from 7 using a number line to find the answer of −8.
2 **16.41** Refer to Test 18 Q3 on adding decimals using column addition.
3 **65.23** Use the place value column from Test 2 Q3. 3 needs to have a value of $\frac{3}{100}$, the same as 3 hundredths. Place the 3 in the hundredths column first, then add the rest of the numbers in the preceding columns, making sure their order remains the same.
4 **C** The money needs to be calculated in a ratio of £1.00 to £.1.50. When completing ratio questions, it is important to keep the information given in the same order. Najib is given £6.00, so work out how many lots of £1.50 give a total of £6.00: 4 × £1.50 = £6.00. Multiply £1.00 by 4 as well to find out how much money Nazar gets: 4 × £1.00 = £4.00.
5 **A** Refer to Test 10 Q4 on multiples. Write out a list of the multiples of each number, using knowledge of times tables. Look for the lowest number that appears in each list.
6 **E** Refer to Test 5 Q3 on short division. 204 ÷ 6 = 34
7 **C** Percent means per 100; a percentage is a number out of 100, therefore 70% is the same as 70 out of 100, which can be written as $\frac{70}{100}$. The marks were out of 50 so find the equivalent fraction with a denominator of 50 by dividing both numbers by 2: $\frac{35}{50} = \frac{70}{100}$. The numerator is 35, which is the answer.
8 **cm (centimetres)** Use knowledge of the length of items you are familiar with to help choose the correct answer. For example, a pen is about 14 cm long, a 10-year-old child is about 1.3 m, etc.
9 **composite number** Refer to Test 16 Q10 on prime numbers and composite numbers.
10 **C** When making approximations, numbers are rounded. 28 is rounded to 30 and 32 is rounded to 30 also, so option C is the correct answer. Refer to Test 5 Q10 on rounding.

Test 23: Mixed (p31)

1 **4.55, 4.51, 4.5, 4.15, 4.05** Refer to Test 8 Q7 on decimal order. Place the numbers in a grid, ensuring the decimal points are aligned. Add a zero in any gaps after the decimal point, so all numbers have the same amount of decimal places. Descending order means largest number first. Look for the largest number in the first column: if they are all the same, go onto the next column, and so on.

4	•	5	0
4	•	5	5
4	•	1	5
4	•	5	1
4	•	0	5

2 **B** Refer to Test 3 Q7 on acute angles.
3 **64, 72, 80** Use knowledge of the 8 times tables to find multiples of 8. 64, 72 and 80 are the only answers in the 8 times table that are between 63 and 87.
4 **7** Refer to Test 16 Q10 on prime numbers.
5 **E** Some options can be ruled out by seeing that the units will not add up to give an answer of 7. Use column addition to check the total of each viable option. Refer to Test 14 Q4 on column addition.
6 **▲** The pattern shown is a repeating sequence of <▲>>▲. There are 5 shapes repeating, so use knowledge of the 5 times table to count up in fives. 3 × 5 = 15 and every fifth shape is a ▲.
7 **385** 1 hour = 60 minutes and 6 × 60 = 360 minutes (see Test 7 Q9 on column multiplication). Add the remaining 25 minutes to the total: 360 + 25 = 385 (refer to Test 14 Q4 on column addition).
8 **6 or 7** A mobile phone is 15-16cm long and there are 100 cm in 1 metre. 6 × 15 cm = 90 cm and 7 × 15 cm = 105 cm; 6 × 16 cm = 96 cm and 7 × 16 = 112 cm.
9 **mile** 1 mile is approximately 1.6 km, therefore 1 mile is longer.
10 **D** To find the fraction of a number, divide the whole number by the denominator (bottom number) in the fraction: 20 ÷ 10 = 2. If the fraction has a numerator (top number) other than 1, multiply the answer by the numerator: 2 × 3 = 6, therefore 6 children are away ill. Subtract this from 20 to find how many children were left in class: 20 − 6 = 14.

Test 24: Mixed (pp 32–33)

1. **280** Refer to Test 3 Q6 on finding the area of a rectangle and Test 7 Q9 on column multiplication. $35 \times 8 = 280$ m^2.
2. e.g.

   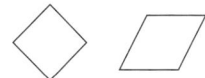

   Parallel lines are always the same distance apart, they never meet or cross. Parallel sides will do the same.
3. **(16 ÷ 8) + (14 + 7) = 23** Refer to Test 20 Q7 on completing calculations with missing operations. The answer to the calculation in each set of brackets needs to be added together to make 23: (16 ÷ 8) = 2 and (14 + 7) = 21, so the equation becomes 2 + 21 = 23, therefore the answer is ÷ and + .
4. **1 hour 37 minutes** Refer to Test 11 Q6 on calculating lengths of time. 17:27 to 18:00 is 33 minutes; 18:00 to 19:00 is 1 hour; and 19:00 to 19:04 is 4 minutes. Add these together = 1 hour 37 minutes.
5. **B** Refer to Test 3 Q4 on symmetry.
6. **8.2** Carefully count the number of millimetres after the number of centimetres shown: this will be the number after the decimal point.

7–8. **Australia, 3** Look for the shortest bar line to find the least visited destination: the line for Australia is the shortest, showing only 4 families. Count the number of bar lines that are higher than 7: Spain, Wales and France.

9. **E** This is a 3D shape, so the unseen faces need to be visualised. Count the number of faces to find its name: there are 8 faces and a 3D shape with 8 faces is an octahedron.
10. Refer to Test 1 Q4 on drawing reflections.

Test 25: Mixed (p 34)

1. **2, 3, 4, 6, 9, 12, 18** Refer to Test 5 Q4 on factors.
2. **250** 1 kg = 1000g, so find $\frac{1}{4}$ of 1000g = 250g.
3. **6790, 6800** Refer to Test 5 Q10 on rounding.
4. **266.67** Refer to Test 2 Q7 on subtracting decimal numbers. 321.56 − 54.89 = 266.67.
5. **A** A hexagonal pyramid has one hexagon-shaped face on the base. There are 6 sides on a hexagon, so the pyramid will have 6 triangular faces from the bottom (joining in a point at the top), so 7 faces altogether. A cube has 6 faces. 7 − 6 = 1
6. **C** 9 out of 12 pieces were eaten (4 + 1 + 2 + 1 + 1 = 9) and this can be written as $\frac{9}{12}$. Subtract $\frac{9}{12}$ from $\frac{12}{12}$ (the whole cake) to find how much is left ($\frac{12}{12} - \frac{9}{12} = \frac{3}{12}$). $\frac{3}{12}$ is the same as 3 ÷ 12 = $\frac{1}{4}$ or 0.25 (refer to Test 5 Q9 on changing fractions into decimals). 0.25 = 25%
7. **D 103m** 7 + 23 + 5 + 15 + 25 + 12 + 16 = 103
8. **x = (5, 5), Ø = (3, 1), ¥ = (2, 8)** See Test 1 Q3 on coordinates.
9. **95 r 3** Use short division. There is a remainder (r) of 3 as 6 does not go into 573 exactly.
10. **D** Draw a number line and count back from 6 to −18. Or, as a calculation: 6 − −18 = 6 + 18 = 24.

Test 26: Mixed (p 35)

1. **798** See to Test 3 Q5 on multiplying by powers of 10.
2. **C** Any fraction that is less than the equivalent of one half will have a numerator that is less than half of the denominator. For example, $\frac{4}{8}$ is the equivalent of $\frac{1}{2}$, therefore $\frac{1}{8}$, $\frac{2}{8}$ and, $\frac{3}{8}$ are less than $\frac{1}{2}$. C is the only option that shows this in all of its fractions.
3. **D** Add 23 and 41 and divide the answer by 2: 23 + 41 = 64; 64 ÷ 2 = 32.

4–5. **10, $\frac{1}{5}$** 2 × 5 = 10 cm^2. The large rectangle has an area of 50 cm^2 (5 × 10), so 10 cm^2 out of 50 cm^2 is shaded; $\frac{10}{50}$ can be simplified to $\frac{1}{5}$.

6. **LIKELY** Refer to Test 4 Q2 on probability.
7. **661.5** 299.6 + 32.8 + 329.1 = 661.5.
8. **e.g. ml = a spoon of medicine, m = the length of a room** Millilitres and litres are used for liquid measurements (capacity) and millimetres, centimetres and metres are used to measure length.
9. **B** Begin with the amount of mice Paws catches (14). Scamp catches one more than Paws = 15 mice. Paws catches double the amount that Spot catches (7). 14 + 15 + 7 = 36
10. Refer to Test 15 Q3 on changing 24-hour clock to analogue and drawing hands on a clock face. 17 − 12 = 5, so the hour hand is just past 5. 4 on the clock face represents 20 minutes, so the minute hand points to 4.

Test 27: Mixed (pp 36–37)

1. **−0.5** Refer to Test 2 Q2 on negative numbers. First, add the numbers to the longer lines on the diagram. Each of the smaller lines is half-way between each number, representing an increment of 0.5.

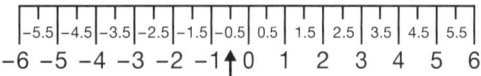

2. **7.84, 0.0784** The numbers have been divided by 10 each time to give the sequence. 78.4 ÷ 10 = 7.84, 0.784 ÷ 10 = 0.0784.

3–4. **0 and 1, 18** Each year since he was born is on the x axis and his height on the y axis. Look for the section of the line with the greatest increase between two years: between the age of 0 and 1 he grew from 52 cm to 76 cm = 24 cm. At the age of 7, he was 124 cm and had grown to 142 cm by the time he was aged 10: 142 − 124 = 18 cm.

5. **e.g.**

See Test 1 Q10 on perpendicular lines.

6. **E** Refer to Test 3 Q4 on symmetry.
7. **B** Move the page round as you work through the directions. Remember that a 90° turn is the same as a quarter turn and to always count on from the next square, not the one you are 'standing' on.
8. *A shape showing two acute and two obtuse interior angles e.g.*

Refer to Test 3 Q7 on acute and obtuse angles.

9. **2309.7** Refer to Test 5 Q2 on subtracting decimal numbers. 2333.0 − 23.3 = 2309.7
10. **C** Autumn started on September 15th so you must include this day in your calculations. in September has 30 days, so 15th to 30th September is 16 days. Add on 31 days in October and the 10 days for November: 16 + 31 + 10 = 57.

Test 28: Mixed (p 38)

1. **D** The front of a cereal box is approximately 35 cm by 25 cm, which is closest to 800 cm².
2. **9 times table**
3. **203 015** Write the numbers in a place value grid using zeros as 'place-holders'. For example, the number 102 needs a 0 otherwise it becomes 12, a completely different number.
4. **C** Count the number of millimetres after the number of centimetres to give the number after the decimal point.
5. *Triangle with sides of different lengths e.g.*

6. **11 000** Refer to Test 5 Q10 on rounding.
7. **E** Multiples of 3 can be divided by 3 exactly. Use your knowledge of 3-, 6-, 9- and 12-times tables to identify numbers which divide by 3.
8. **136 cm** The mode is the number that occurs the most often.
9. **0.3** 3 ÷ 10 = 0.3. Refer to Test 5 Q9 on converting fractions into decimals.
10. **102** First solve 34 × 6 (refer to Test 7 Q9), then divide the answer by 2 (refer to Test 5 Q3). 34 × 6 = 204; 204 ÷ 2 = 102

Test 29: Mixed (p 39)

1. **56** Use short division to complete the sum (refer to Test 5 Q3). 448 ÷ 8 = 56
2. **227** Angles around a point always add up to 360°, so subtract 133 from 360.
3. $\frac{31}{9}$ Refer to Test 20 Q2 on converting a mixed number into an improper fraction. 3 wholes is $\frac{27}{9}$; $\frac{27}{9} + \frac{4}{9} = \frac{31}{9}$.
4. **673 781, 687 371, 736 817, 736 818, 778 316** Refer to Test 2 Q8 on comparing numbers. Ascending order means smallest first, largest last.
5. **A** See Test 5 Q4 on factors.
6. **C** A cylinder has a circular face at each end and a curved face which joins them together.
7. **Approximately 50** The jar is shown as approximately $\frac{1}{5}$ full. $\frac{1}{5}$ of 250 is 250 ÷ 5 = 50.
8. **B** The perimeter of a shape is the total length around the outside. A rectangle has two widths the same size and two lengths the same size, so divide 90 m by 2 to get the total of one width + one length (90 ÷ 2 = 45). The rectangle is twice as long as it is wide, so this is in a ratio of 2 : 1. Add the numbers in the ratio together to find out how much to divide 45 by (2 + 1 = 3 and 45 ÷ 3 = 15). Multiply each of the numbers in the ratio to find the measurements: 2 × 15 = 30 (length) and 1 × 15 = 15 (width). Or, complete as an algebraic equation: 2x + 2x + x + x = 90 m, therefore 6x = 90 m (2x + 2x + x + x = 6x). 90 ÷ 6 = 15, so x = 15 and 2x = 30.

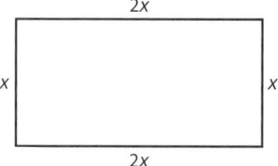

9 **1111** There are 1000 years in one millennium, 100 years in one century and 10 years in one decade: 1000 + 100 + 10 + 1 = 1111.

10 **C** 1000 millilitres = 1 litre and 1000 g = 1 kg, so divide both numbers by 1000 (refer to Test 2 Q3 on dividing by powers of ten).
1500 ÷ 1000 = 1.5 = $1\frac{1}{2}$; 370 ÷ 1000 = 0.370 = 0.37.

Test 30: Mixed (pp 40–41)

1–3

	Number of stars			
	Panthers	Cheetahs	Lions	Tigers
Terms 1 & 2	123	114	105	121
Terms 3 & 4	108	120	116	109
Terms 5 & 6	114	120	114	108
Total	345	354	335	338

Cheetahs, 114 Use the information given in each column and the total amounts to fill in the blank spaces: for the Panthers, 354 – 123 – 108 = 114; for the Lions 335 – 116 – 114 = 105; and for the Tigers 121 + 109 + 108 = 338. The Cheetahs have the largest total, so they won the cup. The mode is the number that occurs the most often: 114.

4 **75p or £0.75** Round £2.95 to £3.00 and multiply by 15: £3 × 15 = £45.00. When rounding, 5p was added for each roll, so 15 × 5p = 75p (£0.75), need to be deducted from £45.00: this is the change Samir received.

5 **B** Refer to Test 1 Q3 on coordinates.

6 **E** Convert the fraction into a decimal by dividing the numerator by the denominator: 34 ÷ 100 = 0.34. Refer to Test 2 Q3 on dividing by powers of ten.

7 **false** 25.6 × 100 = 2560 and 256 × 10 = 2560, they are equal. Refer to Test 3 Q5 on multiplying by powers of 10.

8 Refer to Test 3 Q4 on symmetry.

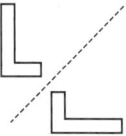

9 *A letter with two lines of symmetry, e.g. H, I, X.* Refer to Test 3 Q4 on symmetry.

10 ▲ The sequence is ▲▲●●■▲, a repeating pattern of 7 shapes. 35 is a multiple of 7 (7 × 5 = 35) so every 7th shape will be the same, a ▲.

Puzzle 1 (page 42)

Each separate number sentence must total 237, e.g. (100 × 2) + (80 ÷ 2) – 3. Follow the rules of BIDMAS: calculations in the brackets are completed first, followed by indices (square roots, square numbers, cubed numbers, etc.), followed by division, multiplication, addition then subtraction. For instance, in the example 200 + (10 × 4) – 3, the calculation in the brackets is completed first and it becomes 200 + 40 – 3 = 237. To create calculations, think of different ways to calculate 200, 30 and 7, then write the calculations together, using brackets where necessary. For example, 100 × 2 = 200, 60 ÷ 2 = 30 and 3 + 4 = 7 and this can be written as (100 × 2) + (60 ÷ 2) + (3 + 4) = 237.

Puzzle 2 (page 43)

9 triangles (1 large, 4 medium and 4 small) Begin by counting the smaller triangles, then the medium-sized triangles (including the one that surrounds the 4 smaller ones) and finally the large triangle surrounding them all.

Separate the large rectangle into 4 smaller rectangles. As well as the four shown, the top two rectangles form one long rectangle, as do the bottom two rectangles. In addition to this, the two rectangles on the left form a rectangle, as do the two on the right. Along with the large rectangle around the outside, a total of 9 rectangles.

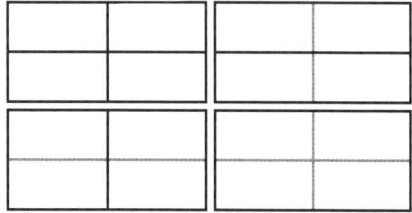

Puzzle 3 (page 44)

Start

40 (8x5)	22 (2x11)	36 (6x6)	54 (9x9)	13	51	69	101
3	41	53	12 (3x4)	127	107	11	61
109	48 (6x8)	100 (10x10)	49 (7x7)	37	32 (8x4)	4 (2x2)	56 (7x8)
29	25 (5x5)	131	53	5	16 (2x8)	67	35 (7x5)
17	63 (7x9)	73	21 (7x3)	49 (7x7)	90 (9x10)	19	72 (9x8)
89	77 (11x7)	9 (3x3)	33 (3x11)	31	19	50 (5x10)	44 (11x4)
7	47	103	61	83	97	42 (6x7)	71
23	59	113	79	137	11	24 (3x8)	44 (4x11)

Finish

Use knowledge of times tables and prime numbers to complete this puzzle: any prime numbers cannot be used as they do not have answers in any times tables other than 1. Refer to Test 16 Q10 on prime numbers.

Puzzle 4 (page 45)

For the pattern to be symmetrical, crosses either side of the bold line need to be a mirror image of one another. Use the squares to count along, upwards and downwards to help position the crosses correctly.

		X	X	X	X		
	X					X	
X	X		X	X		X	X
X	X		X	X		X	X
	X					X	
		X	X	X	X		

Puzzle 5 (page 46)

When using Roman Numerals, use knowledge of how the numbers 1 to 10 are represented to help write larger numbers: 1 = I; 2 = II; 3 = III; 4 = IV; 5 = V; 6 = VI; 7 = VII; 8 = VIII; 9 = IX; and 10 = X. The number 4 is written as IV, to show 1 less than V by placing I in front of V, so 40 will be XL (10 less than 50), 400 will be CD (100 less than 500), and so on. The number 9 is written as IX, to show 1 less than X, then 90 will be XC (10 less than 100), 900 will be CM (10 less than 1000), and so on. The number 6 is VI, to show V plus 1 by placing the I after the V. Therefore, 60 is LX (50 plus 10), 600 is DC (500 plus 100), and so on. The digits 7 and 8 follow the same pattern.

1 **XII** 12 months (10 = X; 2 = II)
2 **CCCLXV** 365 days (300 = CCC; 60 = LX; 5 = V)
3 **CLXXX** 60 minutes in 1 hour, 3 × 60 = 180 (100 = C; 80 = LXXX)
4 **XXXI** 31 days (30 = XXX; 1 = I)
5 **MM** 1000 millilitres in 1 litre, 2 × 1000 = 2000 (1000 = M, so 2000 = MM)
6 **XXVI** 26 (20 = XX; VI = 6)

III 21 ÷ 7 = 3
L 10 × 5 = 50
MDCLXXVI 1600 + 76 = 1676 (1000 = M; 600 = DC; 70 = LXX; and 6 = VI)
DCCCXXX 1000 − 170 = 830 (800 = DCCC; 30 = XXX)

6

Draw the reflection of this shape in the mirror line.

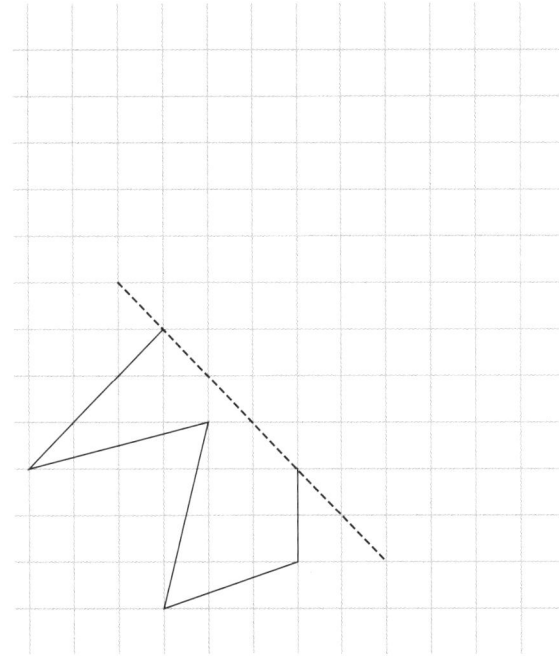

7

A bag of guinea pig food weighs 3.6 kg. How much would 1 000 bags weigh?

Circle the answer.

A .36 kg

B 36 kg

C 360 kg

D 3 600 kg

E 36 000 kg

8

Which of the following shapes are regular polyhedrons?

Circle the answer.

a 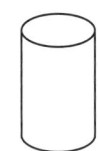   b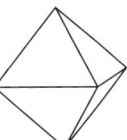

c 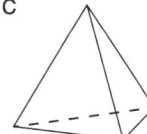   d

e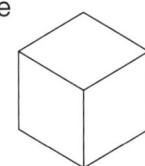

A a, b, e

B b, c, e

C b, e

D d

E a, e

9

Look at this number line.

Estimate the whole number the arrow is pointing to.

_____

10

Write this fraction as a percentage.

$\frac{44}{50}$ = _____ %

TEST 19: Mixed

Test time: 0 — 5 — 10 minutes

1

Draw a straight line between the dots. How long is the line? _____ cm

•

                                                  •

2

_____ km = **400 m**

3

How many times can you subtract 9 from 1260?

Circle the answer.

A 100 **B** 120 **C** 140 **D** 160 **E** 180

4

On Wednesday 24th October, Sanjeev was told he had been chosen to play in a football tournament on the 2nd November. On which day of the week does the tournament take place?

Circle the answer.

A Monday   **B** Tuesday
C Wednesday   **D** Thursday
E Friday

5

Florence spent 8 hours of Tuesday at school.

What fraction of the whole day was she at school? _____

6

What is the difference in temperature between −8°C and 18°C?

_____

7

Which of the following options shows four multiples of 8?

Circle the answer.

A 12, 16, 24, 30   **B** 48, 56, 64, 70
C 8, 18, 28, 38   **D** 40, 56, 72, 88
E 1, 2, 4, 8

8

Write a number story that reflects the following, 237 ÷ 3 = 79

_____
_____
_____
_____

9

Write the time shown on the analogue clock on the 24-hour clock.

 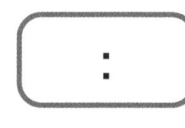

10

Which of these shapes is a regular polygon?

Circle the answer.

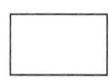 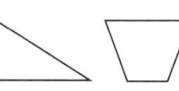 

A   **B**   **C**   **D**   **E**

Total

Test 20: Mixed

1. Complete this sequence.

_____ 5 11 23 _____ 95

2. Convert this mixed number into an improper fraction.

$2\frac{3}{5}$ = _____

3-5. Complete the frequency table.

Spelling test survey showing children in Class 5D with 90% or over		
Week	Tally	Total
1									
2		9
3												
4		4

Represent the information from the frequency table as a bar chart.

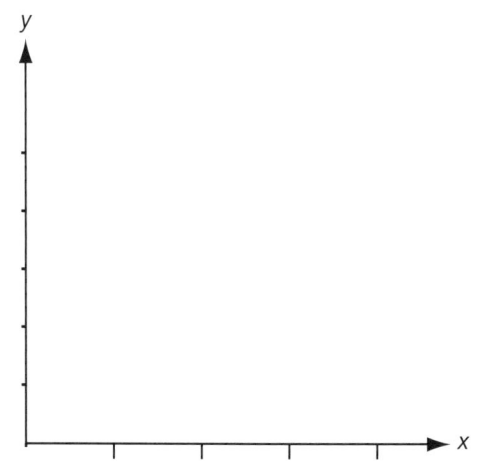

6. Dan made a run for his puppy in the garden. It measured 7 m by 3 m. As his puppy grew he needed a larger area so Dan extended the run to 9 m by 3 m. What area was the run increased by?

_____ m²

7. Add the missing signs to make this correct.

(9 _____ 4) _____ 8 = 44

8. Write thirty-six hundredths as a decimal fraction.

_____

9-10. Is angle x acute or obtuse?

_____

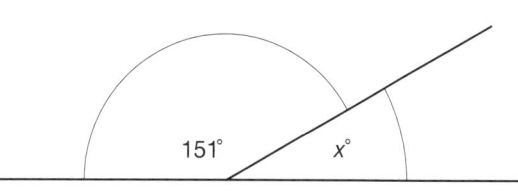

What is the missing angle?

_____°

Test 21: Mixed

Test time: 0 — 5 — 10 minutes

1

Circle the option that shows two perpendicular lines.

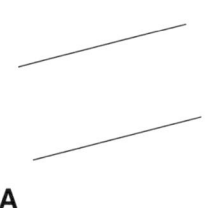

A   B

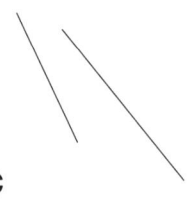

C   D

E

2

Translate this shape 3 units to the left.

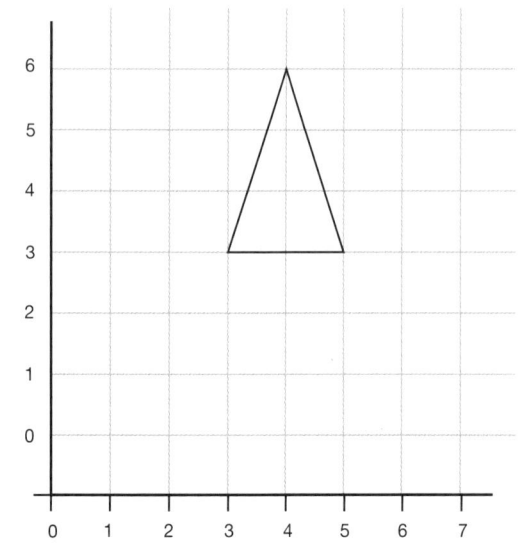

3

Plot these points on this grid.
Then join up the points.
(2, 3)
(3, 7)
(6, 2)

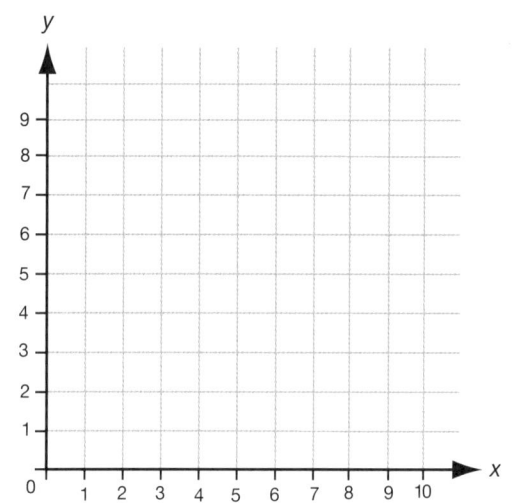

4

Name the triangle you have drawn in Question 3.

_____

5

What number am I thinking of?
If you divide it by 8, then add 17 the answer is 22.

_____

6

Draw the net of this shape.

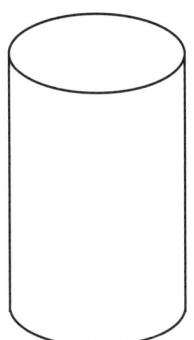

8

Look at the line graph. Answer the questions.

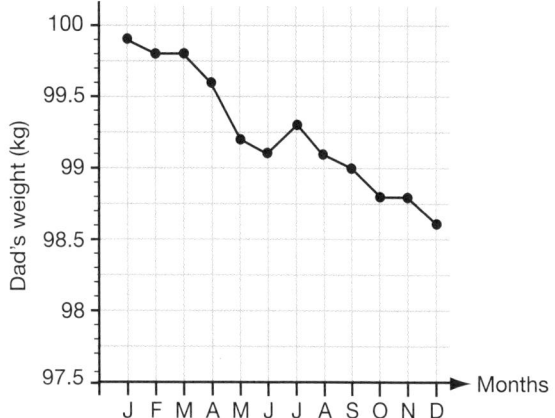

Between which two months did Dad lose the most weight?

_____

How much weight did Dad lose in total?

_____ kg

7

Which shape has only two lines of symmetry?
Circle the answer.

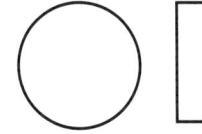  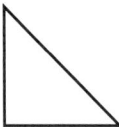

A   B   C

D   E

9

Write the answer to 6.823 × 7

_____

10

Write in words, the largest number you can make using these digits:

5 5 6 7 3 5

_____
_____
_____

Test 22: Mixed

Test time: 0 – 10 minutes

1 The temperature is 7°C. Overnight it falls by 15 degrees. What temperature does it fall to?
Circle the answer.
A −15°C   B −8°C   C −7°C   D 7°C   E 8°C

2
```
   9.56
+  6.85
———
```

3 Rewrite this number adding a decimal point so the 3 has a value of $\frac{3}{100}$.
6523 _____

4 Each week Nazar is given £1.00 pocket money and Najib, his older brother, is given £1.50. For every £6.00 Najib is given, how much does Nazar get?
Circle the answer.
A £2   B £3   C £4   D £4.50   E £5.50

5 What is the lowest common multiple of 2, 3 and 4?
Circle the answer.
A 12   B 24   C 9   D 10   E 20

6 After a strong autumnal wind many apples fell in an orchard. 204 apples were collected and shared between 6 families. How many apples did each family receive?
Circle the answer.
A 8   B 10   C 12   D 24   E 34

7 Sam achieved 70% in her maths test. The test was out of 50.
What mark out of 50 did Sam get?
Circle the answer.
A 25   B 30   C 35   D 40   E 45

8 Which unit of measure would you use to measure the distance a snail has moved in a minute?
_____

9 Is the number 27 a prime number or a composite number?
_____

10 Circle the best approximation for 28 × 32.
A 30 × 32   B 29 × 32   C 30 × 30   D 28 × 30   E 28 × 31

Test 23: Mixed

Test time: 0 — 5 — 10 minutes

1 List these decimals in descending order.

4.5   4.55   4.15   4.51   4.05

_____ _____ _____ _____ _____

2

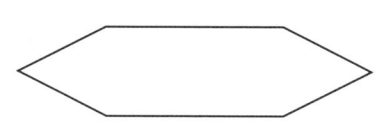

How many acute angles can be found in this shape?
Circle the answer.

A 1   **B** 2   **C** 3   **D** 4   **E** 5

3 Which three numbers between 63 and 87 are exactly divisible by 8?

_____ _____ _____

4 How many prime numbers are there between the numbers 20 and 50?

_____

5 Which three consecutive numbers add up to 57?
Circle the answer.

A 19, 20, 21
B 17, 18, 19
C 20, 21, 22
D 16, 17, 18
E 18, 19, 20

6 Look carefully at this sequence. What will be the 15th symbol?

< ▲ > > ▲ < ▲ >

_____

7 The school day at Minety Primary School lasts for 6 hours 25 minutes.
How many minutes is this altogether?
_____ minutes

8 Estimate how many mobile phones, when placed so the shorter sides are touching, will make 1 metre. _____
Explain how you came up with your answer.

_____
_____
_____
_____
_____

9 Which is the longer distance, a mile or a kilometre? _____

10 Class 5 has 20 pupils. How many pupils are there in class if $\frac{3}{10}$ of them are away ill?
Circle the answer.

A 3   **B** 6   **C** 12   **D** 14   **E** 17

Test 24: Mixed

Test time: 0 — 5 — 10 minutes

1

Find the area of this swimming pool.

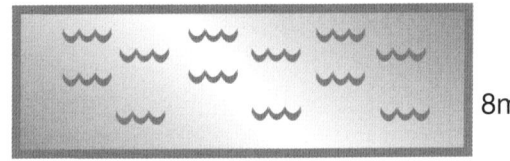

35m

8m

_____ m²

2

Without drawing a square or a rectangle, draw a polygon with two pairs of parallel sides.

3

Add the missing signs to make this correct.

(16 _____ 8) + (14 _____ 7) = 23

4

A train leaves Paddington station at 17:27. It arrives in Kemble at 19:04.
How long does the journey take?

_____

5

In one of these groups the letters have 0, 1 and 2 lines of symmetry.
Circle the answer.

A F, G, H

B Q, E, X

C I, M, T

D Z, C, B

E J, H, X

6

Draw a straight line between the dots. How long is the line you have drawn?

•

•

_____ cm

7-8

This bar line chart shows the results of a holiday survey.

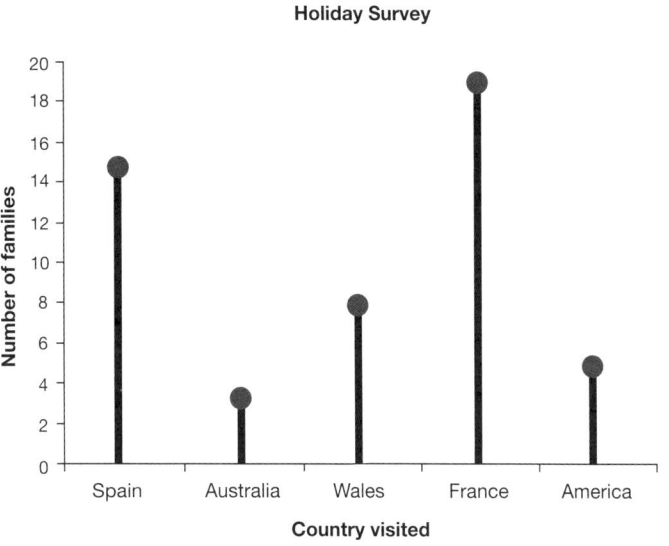

Which destination was visited by the least number of families?

_____

How many destinations were visited by 7 families or more?

_____

9

What is this 3-D shape? Circle the answer.

A tetrahedron

B icosahedron

C hexagonal pyramid

D prism

E octahedron

10

Draw the reflection of this shape in the mirror line.

Time for a break! Go to Puzzle Page 45

Test 25: Mixed

Test time: 0 — 5 — 10 minutes

1 List the factors of 36. Two have already been done for you.

1 ___ ___ ___ ___ ___ ___ ___ 36

2 $\frac{1}{4}$ kg = _____ g

3 Round 6791 to the nearest 10 and 100.

___ ___

4 Subtract 54.89 from 321.56 _____

5 How many more faces does a hexagonal pyramid have compared to a cube? Circle the answer.

A 1   B 2   C 3   D 4   E 5

6 Mum cut a cake into 12 equal pieces. After school her four children had a slice each and she had one too. Later a neighbour called in and ate two slices. When the babysitter and her friend were hungry they ate a slice each. What percentage of the cake was left at the end of the day? Circle the answer.

A 5%   B 10%   C 25%   D 35%   E 50%

7

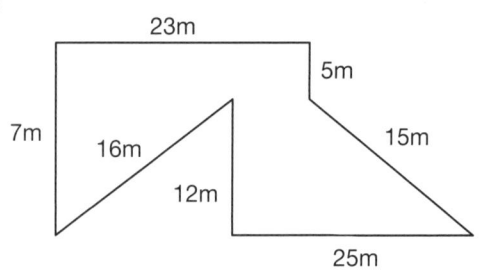

Find the perimeter of this irregular shape. Circle the answer.

A 101 m   B 114 m   C 102 m
D 103 m   E 109 m

8 Write the coordinates of the points marked on the grid.

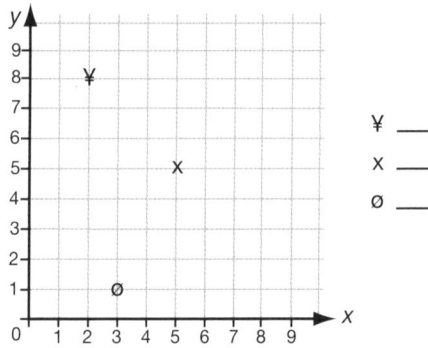

¥ _____
× _____
ø _____

9 6)573   _____ r _____

10 The temperature a freezer should be set at is −18°C. If the temperature of a freezer is 6°C, how much does the temperature need to decrease? Circle the answer.

A 6°C   B 12°C   C 18°C
D 24°C   E 36°C

Test 26: Mixed

1 Multiply 7.98 by 100 _____

2 Circle the answer that shows a group of fractions which are each less than a half.

A $\frac{7}{10}$ $\frac{5}{9}$ $\frac{2}{5}$ B $\frac{1}{2}$ $\frac{3}{7}$ $\frac{2}{5}$

C $\frac{5}{12}$ $\frac{2}{5}$ $\frac{4}{10}$ D $\frac{1}{5}$ $\frac{4}{6}$ $\frac{3}{5}$

E $\frac{4}{9}$ $\frac{2}{4}$ $\frac{1}{3}$

3 What number is halfway between 23 and 41?
Circle the answer.

A 29   B 30   C 31   D 32   E 33

4-5

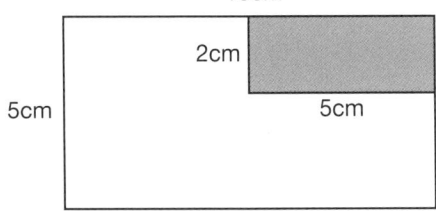

Find the area of the rectangle that is shaded. _____ cm²

What fraction of the large rectangle is shaded? _____

6 Circle the word you would match with the statement

 'I will see fireworks on or around 5th November'

CERTAIN   **LIKELY**

UNLIKELY   **IMPOSSIBLE**

7 The Roberts family were travelling to a family wedding. They drove 299.6 miles up to Newcastle on Friday, a total of 32.8 miles to and from the wedding on Saturday and 329.1 miles returning home via a Roman villa on Sunday.
How many miles did they travel in total?
_____ miles

8 Write an item you would use each of the following units to measure.

millilitres = _____

metres = _____

9 Three young cats enjoy catching mice. Over a week Paws catches double the mice that Spot catches and Scamp catches one more than Paws. Paws catches 14 mice. How many mice are caught in total? Circle the answer.

A 28   B 36   C 38   D 42   E 49

10 Sharma arrives home from a school trip at 17:20. Show this time on the clock face.

Test 27: Mixed

Test time: 0 – 5 – 10 minutes

1

What number is the arrow pointing to?

_____

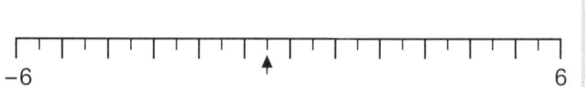

2

Fill in the missing numbers in this sequence.

784   78.4 _____   **0.784** _____

3-4

Records were kept of Jacob's height since he was born. He drew the results on the following line graph.

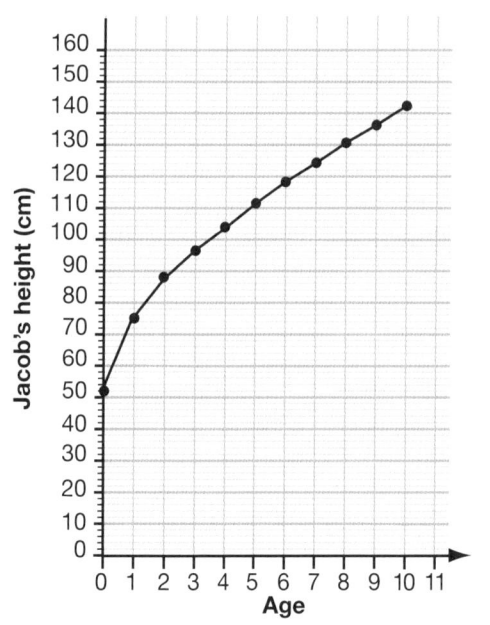

Between which two years did Jacob's height increase the most? _____

How many centimetres has Jacob grown in the last three years? _____ cm

5

Draw a line perpendicular to this line.

6

How many lines of symmetry does this shape have?
Circle the answer.

A 1
B 2
C 3
D 4
E 5

7

Guide your dog to the park avoiding all objects on the way.

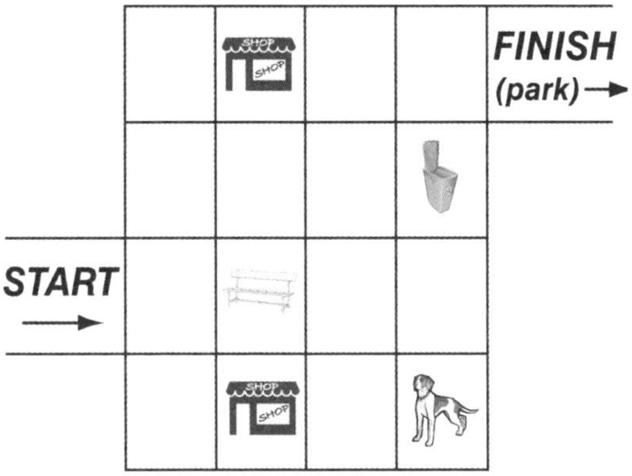

Circle the correct instructions.

A FORWARD 1, TURN LEFT 90°,
FORWARD 2, TURN RIGHT 90°,
FORWARD 4

B FORWARD 1, TURN LEFT 90°,
FORWARD 1, TURN RIGHT 90°,
FORWARD 2, TURN LEFT 90°,
FORWARD 1, TURN RIGHT 90°,
FORWARD 2

C FORWARD 1, TURN LEFT 90°,
FORWARD 1, TURN RIGHT 90°,
FORWARD 3

D FORWARD 1, TURN LEFT 90°,
FORWARD 1, TURN RIGHT 90°,
FORWARD 2, TURN RIGHT 90°,
FORWARD 1, TURN LEFT 90°,
FORWARD 2

8

Draw a shape with two acute interior angles and two obtuse interior angles.

9

2333 − 23.3 = _____

10

If autumn started on September 15th and ended on November 10th, how many days did autumn last?
Circle the answer.

A 55 days

B 56 days

C 57 days

D 58 days

E 59 days

Test 28: Mixed

Test time: 0 — 5 — 10 minutes

1 What is the approximate area of the front of a cereal box?
Circle the answer.

A 0.8 cm²   B 8 cm²   C 80 cm²
D 800 cm²   E 8000 cm²

2 Which multiplication table contains the following sequence of numbers?

54   63   72   81   _____

3 Write 'two hundred and three thousand and fifteen' in numbers. _____

4 Measure this line exactly. Circle the answer.
_____

A 1.8cm   B   2 cm   C 2.8 cm
D 3.2cm   E   3.5 cm

5 Draw a scalene triangle.

6 Write 10 901 to the nearest 1000.
_____

7 Which of these options shows three multiples of 12?
Circle the answer.

A 24, 56, 96
B 34, 72, 86
C 100, 108, 120
D 37, 61, 109
E 48, 84, 96

8 Find the mode of these children's heights.
_____

135 cm   148 cm   136 cm   143 cm
148 cm   136 cm   139 cm   136 cm

9 Write $\frac{3}{10}$ as a decimal. _____

10
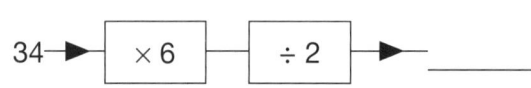

34 → × 6 → ÷ 2 → _____

Test 29: Mixed

Test time: 0 — 5 — 10 minutes

1 Divide four hundred and forty-eight by eight. _____

2 Calculate the missing angle.

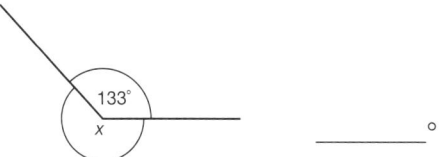

_____ °

3 Write $3\frac{4}{9}$ as an improper fraction.

_____

4 Write these numbers in ascending order.
673 781   736 817   687 371   778 316   736 818

_____ _____ _____ _____ _____

5 Circle the group of numbers that are factors of 24.

A 3, 6, 8   B 10, 12, 24   C 8, 16, 24
D 6, 9, 12   E 1, 9, 12

6 How many faces does a cylinder have? Circle the answer.

A 1   B 2   C 3   D 4   E 5

7 This jar holds 250 sweets when it is full. Approximately how many sweets are in the jar now?

_____

8 The perimeter of a playground is 90 m. It is twice as long as it is wide.
What is its width?
Circle the answer.

A 9m   B 15m   C 18m   D 30m   E 60m

9 Add together one millennium, one century, one decade and one year.

_____ years

10 Circle the equivalent measurements.
1500 millilitres and 370 grams is the same as…

A 15 ℓ and 3.7 kg   B 1.5 ℓ and 3.7 kg
C $1\frac{1}{2}$ ℓ and 0.37 kg   D 1.5 ℓ and 0.037 kg
E 15 ℓ and 0.37 kg

TEST 30: Mixed

Test time: 0 — 5 — 10 minutes

1-3

Horndean Primary School has four mixed year teams. Throughout the school year each team collects stars for good work, being helpful, winning races on sports day etc. At the end of the year a cup is awarded to the winning team.

Complete the table.

	Number of stars			
	Panthers	Cheetahs	Lions	Tigers
Terms 1 & 2	123	114		121
Terms 3 & 4	108	120	116	109
Terms 5 & 6		120	114	108
Total	345	354	335	

Which team won the cup? _____

Find the mode of stars awarded in any period.

_____

4

Samir bought 15 filled rolls costing £2.95 each. How much change did he get from £45.00?

_____

5

Circle the answer that correctly lists the three marked coordinates.

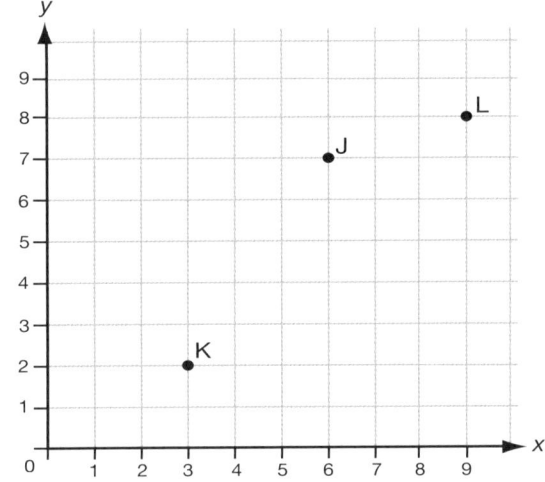

A J (6, 7) K (2, 3) L (9, 8)

B J (6, 7) K (3, 2) L (9, 8)

C J (6, 7) K (9, 8) L (3, 2)

D J (7, 6) K (2, 3) L (9, 8)

E J (7, 6) K (3, 2) L (9, 8)

6

Circle the decimal equal to $\frac{34}{100}$.

A 3.4   B 34.1   C 3.41   D 34.0   E 0.34

7

Is this statement **true** or **false**?

$(25.6 \times 100) < (256 \times 10)$ _____

8

Draw the reflection of this shape in the mirror line.

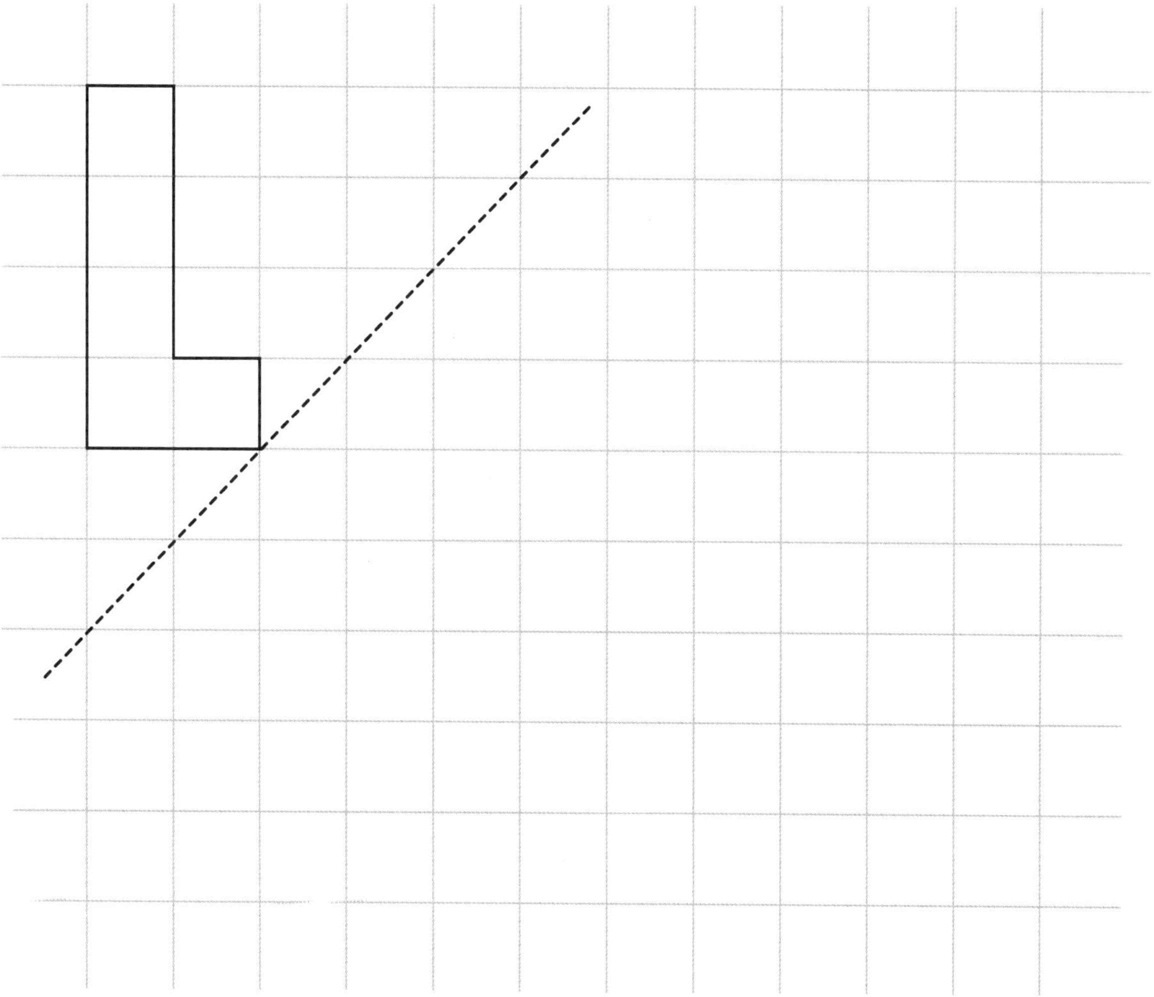

9

Draw a letter with two lines of symmetry.

10

What shape will be 35th in this sequence?

▲ ▲ ● ● ● ■ ▲ ▲ ▲ ● ● ●

______

Total

Time for a break! Go to Puzzle Page 46 ▸

Puzzle ❶

How many different ways can you find this number?
Remember to use +, −, × and ÷.

200 + (10 × 4) − 3

$$237$$

Puzzle ❷

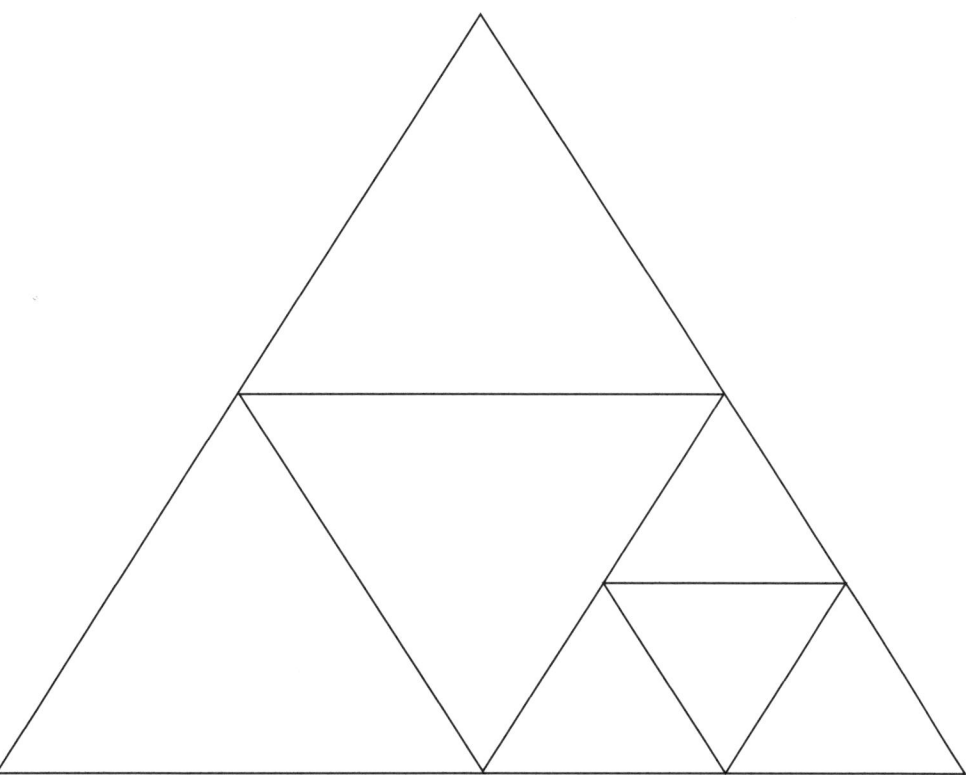

How many triangles can you find in this shape? _____

Now, by adding lines to the outline below, create a shape with nine rectangles.

Puzzle ❸

Can you make your way through the 'times tables' maze?

Find the numbers below that can be made from a times table calculation.

Write the times table calculations below the numbers to complete the challenge!

Rules:
You cannot use the 1 times table.
Each move must be horizontal or vertical, but not diagonal!

Start

40 (8x5)	22	36	54	13	51	69	101
3	41	53	12	127	107	11	61
109	48	100	49	37	32	4	56
29	25	131	53	5	16	67	35
17	63	73	21	49	90	19	72
89	77	9	33	31	19	50	44
7	47	103	61	83	97	42	71
23	59	113	79	137	11	24	44

Finish

Puzzle 4

Complete the pattern.

The bold lines are lines of symmetry.

Use the lines of symmetry and the crosses provided to construct the whole pattern.

Puzzle 5

Roman Numeral Challenge!

I	=	1
V	=	5
X	=	10
L	=	50
C	=	100
D	=	500
M	=	1000

Answer these questions giving the answers in Roman numerals!

1. How many months in a year? _____
2. How many days in a normal year? _____
3. How many minutes in three hours? _____
4. How many days in May? _____
5. How many millilitres in two litres? _____
6. How many letters in the alphabet? _____

Solve these...

XXI ÷ VII = _____

X × V = _____

MDC + LXXVI = _____

M − CLXX = _____

Progress Grid

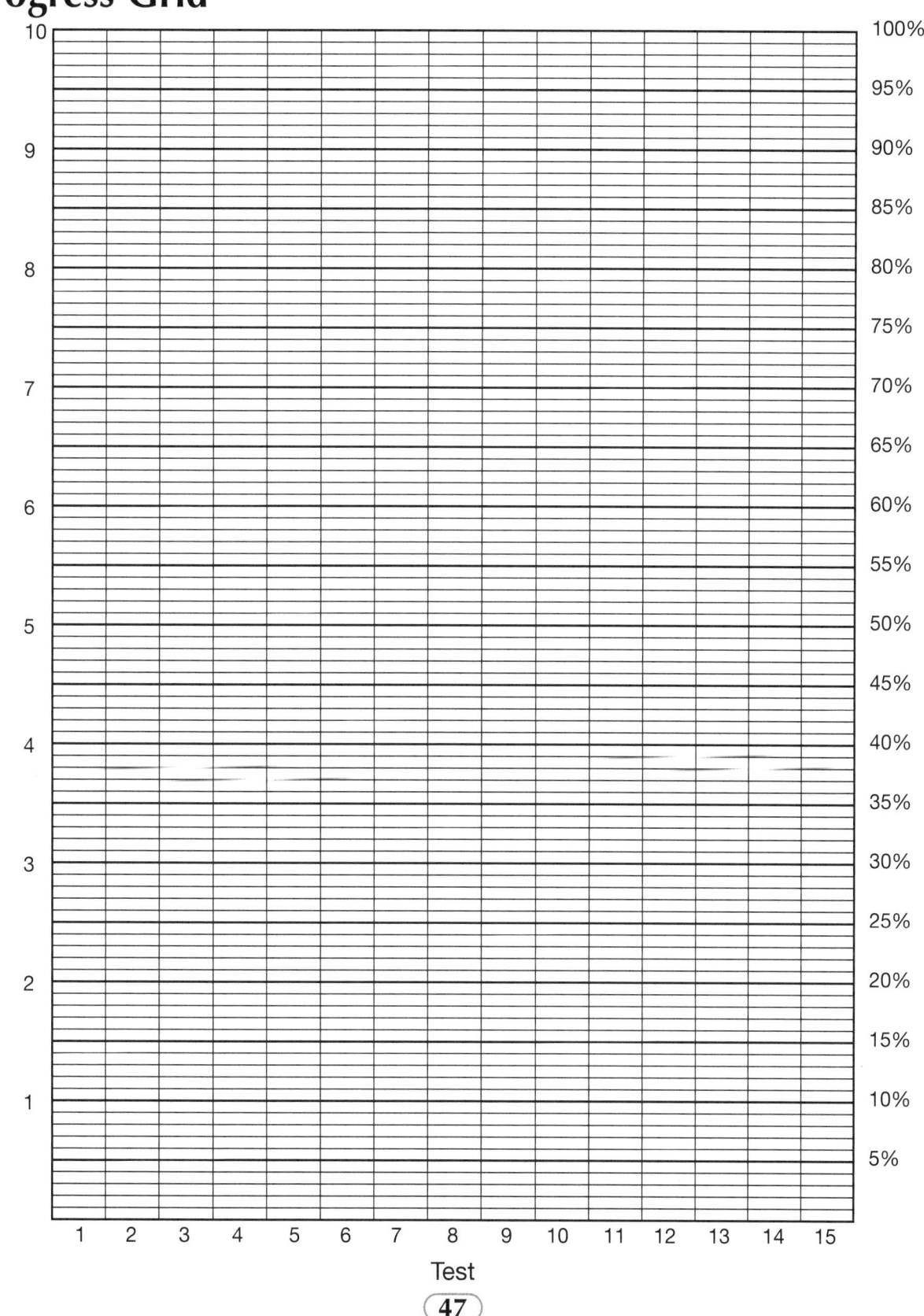

Progress Grid